THREE FINGERS

by Malcolm S. Bates

CLOUDCAP

SEATTLE

THIS BOOK IS DEDICATED TO MY PARENTS

AND HARRY TUCKER

Cover photo by Dick Merfeld
Pilot: Dale Boggs

TABLE OF CONTENTS

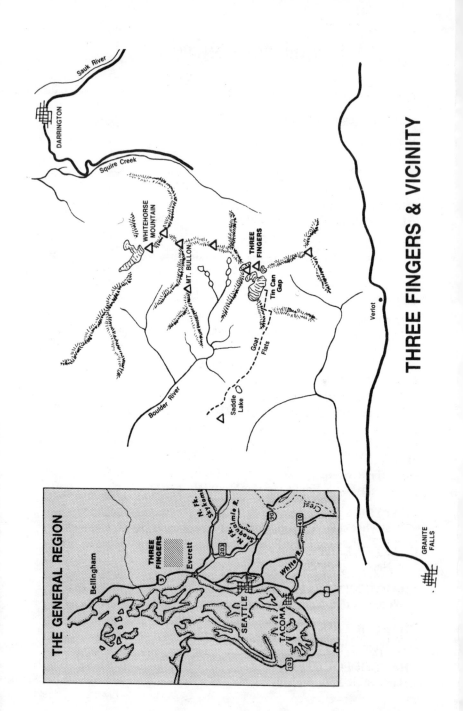

THREE FINGERS & VICINITY

THE GENERAL REGION

FOREWORD

I was four years old in 1955 when I first gazed out the windows of the Three Fingers lookout, accompanied by my father, mother, brother and our beagle. I remember very little of that epic two-week trip from Darrington, up the Boulder Valley, through Goat Flats and on to a four-day stay in the lookout. I do remember Mom not letting me out of her sight. At that independent and wise age of four, I found this a bit annoying. And I remember clutching Susan, my doll, while sitting on top of my father's monstrous pack during our hike up. I also remember hating powdered milk.

I had no inkling of what Three Fingers and the lookout meant to my father, Harry Tucker, and the rest of the family. Nor had I any predilection of what it would come to mean to my cousins, my husband and myself.

Many things in my life have changed in the 32 years since, but the sense of place, of history and of awe that I feel while watching a sunset over the San Juans from Harold Weiss's canvass chair has never deserted me.

On the day I closed the shutters in September of 1986 after a month-long sojourn up there to work on repairs, I knew a chapter in my life had closed. I'd just fulfilled a childhood fantasy of spending at least two weeks up there. But most important, I fully understood for the first time that my family has no corner on the emotions the lookout elicits. The effort, concern and cooperation shown by all who took part in the lookout's renovation, drove home the fact that one need not have a childhood connection to belong to this mountain and the structure that is perched on top of it. At first this realization brought a stab of jealousy to my heart. But it was immediately supplanted by a more mature feeling of thankfulness. The lookout's future is not my responsibility. Its future belongs to a whole group of dedicated people — people who have been enchanted by their visits there.

The book you are about to read is written by one of these people. Mac's love and respect shine through each word of this book he has labored over for the past six years. Only someone as in love with the lookout as I could have devoted the hours of research necessary to flesh out the mountain's colorful history. Not only has he created a book that's enjoyable reading for Three Finger veterans and non-veterans alike; he has also saved a piece of history. When the lookout finally flaps away in that inevitable storm, it and the people who were a part of it will still exist.

— Pat Tucker

ACKNOWLEDGEMENTS

The night I finished my last chapter, I uncorked a bottle of cheap champagne (when this book is published I will haul out the expensive stuff), I began thinking of all the people who have helped make this book a reality. If this were the end of a movie the credits would go on forever. I had so much help. I needed all of it.

The men and women who invited me into their homes to talk about their experiences on Three Fingers were always gracious and patient with a neophyte interviewer whose tape-recorder didn't always work properly. Thanks to Harold Weiss, Kenn Carpenter, Art and Ov Winder, Ed Towne, Robert Craig, Rick McGuire, Phillip Hughes, Jean and Edith Bedal, Kenneth Chapman, Ron Miller, Gertrude Shorrock, Pat Tucker and Bruce Weide. Several people I know only by their handwriting, but their replies to my letters, almost always articulate and witty, were greatly appreciated: Forest Farr, Norval Grigg, Congressman Al Swift, Stan Nurmi, Keith Markwell, Harvey Manning, Dale Cole and William Butler. Harold Engles, Eileen Tucker and Harland Eastwood have been good friends.

My father, William Bates, never wavered in his support for this project, but he also told me early on, when I thought I had the book wrapped up, that there was so much more to say.

Terry Johnson, Dick Hetland and Chris Norment riddled my copy with red pencil marks and made valuable suggestions about style and substance. I am greatly indebted to Andrea Lomas Remington for transcribing hours and hours of taped interviews. Thanks also to Devin Brown who convinced me that the computer isn't a tool of the devil and was patient as I hurled hundreds of silly questions at him.

I would also like to thank those friends and relatives who have climbed Three Fingers with me. In many small and large ways you helped contribute to the book. Brad Knappe always seemed to give me a boost when I needed it most. I am especially grateful to Jim Liming who introduced me to Three Fingers and with whom I have shared some of the best moments a person can have in the mountains, and a few of the worst.

Finally I would like to thank my wife, Carol Roorbach, who was always interested, but always objective. Her support, especially on the down days, was a life-saver. I can't thank her enough.

PREFACE

This book is about a mountain, men and memory. At the core is a snag-toothed peak, uniquely placed on the crest of the Cascades in Washington State, straddling civilization and wilderness, highly visible, yet remote, a dramatic setting for adventure. Around its three fingers spin amazing stories of climbers, miners and men who wanted to place a fire lookout on top of the narrow, sheer-sided south spire, and did just that. The cabin survives today, a fragile monument to hardy men and their dreams; a reminder, too, of a time we will never see again.

The Forest Service, which employed Harold Engles and Harry Bedal, the architects of that amazing project, has changed dramatically. I'm not sure those men would fit into today's Forest Service. Most of the lookout cabins in the North Cascades are gone, as are many of the men who manned them. These men, and women, were endowed with a spirit that is largely absent in today's world; a world which no longer demands of people a physical commitment to daily living. In many ways that is a shame.

Harold Engles, Harland Eastwood, Edith and Jean Bedal found adventure in their daily lives. It was part of the job. Tools were simpler, the landscape harsher and conveniences rare. Even for men like Art Winder and Forest Farr, who climbed mountains for pleasure, the approaches were longer, the equipment primitive and the terrain unknown.

Harold Engles still looks at modern technology with a jaundiced eye, preferring to rely on his two hands. Simplicity and self-reliance remain integral parts of his life. Engles raises a small herd of cows, chops his own firewood and makes and repairs many of his tools and climbing equipment. Harland Eastwood is still an expert carpenter and Bob Craig and his wife work a small vineyard. Age and infirmity have not dulled their zest for adventure.

When I first climbed Three Fingers eighteen years ago, I felt little connection with the mountain's past. As a teenager I was less concerned with the past than the here and now. I didn't have time to reflect on what I considered to be ancient and perhaps irrelevant history.

But I was drawn ineluctably to Three Fingers year after year and every time I hiked up the trail, I became more and more aware of the distant yet resonant echoes of a thousand footsteps — tricouni, tennis shoe and lug sole — pounding the earth alongside me. The lookout cabin was the window on the past and the summit register a very real link with people who had come before me.

To spend a night in the cabin was to sleep, not only on top of the world, removed from its tension and turmoil, but to sleep in a different time, a different world. It was an emotion shared by scores of others who have sought the cabin for shelter.

Preserving the lookout became an overriding concern for me and many other hikers who have stood in front of the cabin at twilight, watched their shadows stretch out over Tin Can Gap, merge with the larger shadows of the cabin to cover Goat Flats and eventually join the immense shadow of the mountain to cover the lowlands and Puget Sound.

Today I am thousands of miles from Three Fingers, but my friend, Dick Hetland, sends me a steady stream of postcards with Three Fingers prominent in them: Three Fingers from the Bainbridge Island ferry, the San Juan Islands, from the Interstate, from Mount Pilchuck. The pictures take me back to the cabin, Goat Flat, Saddle Lake, Harold Engles' living room.

And I am reminded of a passage from Donald Hall's book, *String Too Short to be Saved*. In it he looks at another mountain, in New Hampshire, and writes: "Time elongates as I watch the old mountain. I look into fire and granite that four generations of family eyes have looked at. Sitting on the porch in my great-grandmother's captain's chair, I feel as if our eyes' gazing has braided ribbons of sight that reach from this farm to the slopes five miles away, invisible strands holding generations together, the living and dead and unborn braided together, permanent mountain attached to disappearing flesh."

It was Three Fingers which first led me to Harold Engles, Art Winder, Harry Tucker, Harold Weiss and other extraordinary people. I think the mountain will lead me to other people and other stories. I have been touched by these people more deeply than I ever could have imagined when I first sent tentative inquiries to Harry Tucker and Harold Engles about writing a book. The mountain's touch spans a continent and will be felt for a lifetime.

It is my hope that I have captured not only a bit of the mountain's charm, but conveyed the special nature of the people who explored, climbed and lived on Three Fingers.

CHAPTER ONE

The Road to Three Fingers

*"The rock spires and ice fields of
Three Fingers stand near the west
edge of the North Cascades, rising above
lowlands and saltwater, prominent on
the skyline from as far as Seattle . . .
To get to the trailhead drive the
Mountain Loop highway . . . At 17 miles
from the Mountain Loop Highway are
Tupso Pass and the trailhead, elevation
2800 feet.*

— 101 Hikes in the Cascades

Seventeen miles. Seventeen years. The road to recollection is nearly as long and serpentined as the gravel road that first led us to Three Fingers. I want to recall that trip as an epic poem, but as the vague images loop back through the mind and pass under the withering gaze of an objective eye, they assume an all-too-human quality. Unfortunately I wanted to be super-human.

Combat was the operative metaphor in this teenage boy's life, but I had no stomach for bloody noses and bruises. As a 135-pound defensive tackle on the freshman football team I always looked to make the shirttail tackle rather than lowering my head and bulling into the ballcarrier's solar plexus. I was often dragged 30 yards into the endzone by my intended victim. I looked for opponents who wouldn't fight back. I looked to the mountains. Most often my hiking buddies and I focused our attention on Three Fingers; it would be our Everest. As it happened, we were doomed to lose to an opponent that would not even lift a finger. But we also made a lifelong friend.

On a somewhat less-than-august August morning in 1969, Jim, Craig and I piled into Jim's Chevy II and headed for Three Fingers. The last seventeen miles was on a dirt logging road.

For most of its length the road, with its washboard ruts and small craters, tested not only automotive but human shock absorption. After nearly an hour of jostling, we were eager to climb, and at road's end we jumped out of the car and inhaled several liters of fresh mountain air before pulling gear from the trunk. Ice axes, crampons, a Goldline rope, freshly snowsealed boots, one steel carabiner that hung like a badge from the back of my pack and a healthy dose of teenage bravado: we had everything necessary to mount a successful assault on the Three Fingers Lookout, except the trail.

Fog was draped around us like a stage scrim, giving the trees a gauzy, mysterious and slightly unsettling quality. Before we had a chance to worry, Jim plucked his dog-eared Forest Service map from its plastic ziplock pouch and unfolded it on the hood of the car. The trail was not hard to find on the map; a seismographic pattern of calm and chaos which ended with a wiggle in a patch of brown an inch short of our destination, the abandoned lookout cabin. At the other end the line of dashes was securely anchored to a solid black line, the road. We were obviously here. Where was the trail?

Only slightly daunted, we hoisted packs and hiked fifty yards up the road to where it ended abruptly in a large clearcut. We wandered around the stumps in the fog like ghosts in a Fellini film. Craig stated the obvious, "I think it's somewhere else."

Just as every nationality has its ethnic jokes, so, too, the mountains must have a collection of climber jokes. "How many climbers does it take to find the trail?" . . . three, one to hold the map, one to hold the compass and one to trip over the trail while the other two are arguing over declination. Stumbling aimlessly around the clearcut, in full climbing regalia, I felt like the punchline to a Three Fingers climber's joke.

After a half-hour spent sleuthing through roadside shrubbery, we finally spotted the trail when a young couple emerged from the forest. Assuming the nonchalant pose of a Swiss mountain guide, I asked, "How was the weather at Goat Flats?"

The man answered, "Socked in. We couldn't see a thing." Aha, we were on the right mountain. With recharged confidence we raced for the trailhead, each of us hoping for the lead position. At that age it was important to set the pace, force it until someone cried uncle, hopefully not the leader. Craig and I would fight for the lead, while Jim, content to hang back, tuned in to the mysterious rhythms of the dark forest rather than our race pace. He often inherited the lead somewhere after the first couple of leg-cramping switchbacks.

> *"The trail climbs along the forested*
> *side of the ridge two miles and emerges*
> *into sub-alpine meadows of 3800-foot*
> *Saddle Lake. There is shelter on the*
> *far end of the lake."*

The fog hung in the trees like moss as we hiked to Saddle Lake. The years had not been kind to the trail which was serviceable at best, in danger of sloughing away in many places and very slick in others. Occasional missteps found us unceremoniously dumped on our padded parts. Saddle Lake, which was more lagoon than lake, inspired no picture taking and the sluggish trickle at its outlet did nothing to quench our thirst.

We took a cookie break and discussed the weather and what we might see. Jim talked of lush meadows and superb views at Goat Flats. But what if it rained? We had not brought a tent. Jim reminded us that our goal was the cabin, but if worse came to worst, there was a shelter at Goat Flats.

> *"From the lake the trail ascends*
> *steep slopes above Saddle Lake and in*
> *one mile enters rolling heather. The*
> *meadows are dotted with ponds.*
> *Some two-and-one-half miles from*
> *Saddle Lake the trail reaches the*
> *meadow plateau of 4700-foot Goat Flats*
> *(near the center is a very old and*
> *decrepit log shelter once used as a*
> *patrol cabin). For most hikers the*
> *Flats are far enough, offering a*
> *close-up view of the cliffs and ice*
> *of the North Cascades."*

The trail out of Saddle Lake, for a quarter-mile, was path-puddle, path-puddle, a trail more suited for steeplechasers. There was no way to escape mud until the trail began contouring around the south side to a small meadow, our first break from the gray-green monotony of the fogged-in forest. From that point the path assumed a new character; a primeval trace slowly being reclaimed by nature. Grass sprouted in the trail. We walked, as much as our packs would allow, with a reverence reserved for cathedrals.

Our spirits were lifting with the fog which was now a low

but benign cloud cover. Our arrival at Goat Flats coincided with the sun's first appearance of the day. Sunlight made shiny mirrors of the ponds and added lustre to the pink and white heather which carpeted the Flats. We dropped our packs near the lean-to which was leaning too much. Its dank interior promised an uncomfortable night if "worse came to worst". A peak, illuminated by sun, appeared for a moment and disappeared. Could it have been the south finger? It looked steep. The clouds, like the moving shutter of a camera, closed quickly around the peak and we decided to finish lunch and hit the trail again.

> "For hikers who want more, the trail goes on, traversing meadows and then climbing steeply up a rocky basin to 6400-foot Tin Can Gap, above the Three Fingers Glacier . . ."

The trail from Goat Flats arced across the meadow and into a grove of trees. We emerged from the trees into a steep meadow. The clouds, which had descended once again, muffled sound, and a quartet of Mountaineers, returning from the summit of Three Fingers, was upon us before we could assume acceptable poses. We hopped casually over a log in the trail as the climbers approached. Jim leapt with abandon, caught his boot and splatted face first in the trail, cutting his hand. The climbers passed while we administered clumsy first aid to Jim's hand. Their greeting was perfunctory, as if they had sniffed out amateurs a mile away. We disliked them without even knowing them. Our chagrin soon disappeared as the terrain became more alpine and the warmth of the sun, fighting to break through the clouds, presaged good weather at the Gap.

Below Tin Can Gap the trail zig-zagged through what appeared to be an expertly landscaped rock garden. The swatches of color were dazzling and heightened our giddiness as we approached the Gap; the muted red, pink and lavender of paintbrush, phlox, lupine and penstemon were testament to Mother Nature's good taste in floral arrangement. Tin Can Gap was the perfect resting place and after six miles we were ready to sit back and soak in some scenery.

We had topped the clouds and the tips of numerous peaks were visible to the south as was Whitehorse, a massive sister peak to the north. Three Fingers was still cloaked in clouds. Jim, who had visited the area with Brad, another friend, a couple of weeks earlier, was confident that the snow which had blocked their progress would be gone or inconsequential. Brad had taken a scary slide down a steep snow slope, luckily avoiding cliffs and coming away with only a bruised behind and a broken camera. We peered over the Gap to the Three Fingers Glacier, a broad snow basin with an occasional crevasse. Dropping on to it would be a problem. The snow slope that dropped away from the Gap looked almost convex, much too steep for us. After gulping down some water and raisins, we attacked the upper trail with the confidence of men who had faced the enemy and overwhelmed them. Unfortunately our reverie was broken 200 yards up the trail when we encountered the most precipitous snow slope I had ever contemplated crossing.

> " . . . from Tin Can Gap the way weaves
> along an airy ridge to the foot of the
> pinnacle of the 6854-foot South Peak.
> atop which is perched a lookout cabin
> built in the 1930's. "

The patch of snow was narrow, but the cliffs at its base made my heart palpitate wildly. We were going to have to rope up. Jim and Craig looked to me for advice on the bowline-on-a-coil knot. I was the expert, having taken The Mountaineers' basic climbing course. Heartsick over the infidelities of my first high school girlfriend (at the local roller rink she had skated into the arms of my former best friend and out of my life), I had been plotting revenge when I should have been "sending the rabbit through the hole." I had even failed the easy comprehensive written test. Rather than admitting that I wasn't an official Mountaineer, I bluffed it. Several slip knots later, we were roped to one another and poised, a bit shakily, at the edge of the snow. The slope narrowed between two rock ribs, giving it the appearance of the neck of an hourglass, and opened into a broad basin — a long ride if we slipped. I kicked steps in the crusty snow with pile driving determination, and soon we were halfway across; ahh, it wasn't so bad.

"Falling!" It was Craig . . . sloppy self arrest, snow down my pants, pack pressed against my head, but Jim and I had dug in. We hadn't gone anywhere. Spooked, we stood nervously and shook the snow from our packs and resumed our progress, slowly, delicately.

"Falling!" This time Jim. More snow, cold hands gripping the ice axe vise-like, cursing the snow, my pack, the climb and

Lookout from the upper trail.

Three Fingers from Goat Flats. Lookout is perched on the south peak, second summit from the right.

South peak from Tin Can Gap; lookout on highest point (center).

Jim. Once again we got to our feet and began the trek to the trail which beckoned short yards away . . .

"Whoa, falling!" . . . the words exploded from my mouth. Damn! I was beginning to dislike the prone position. Traveling at this speed, we'd still be on the snow by nightfall. I wondered if we were climbing over our heads. I was just 19. I didn't want to die but, looking back, I didn't want to retrace my steps either. Summoning up energy for the short push to the trail, we literally jumped from snow to solid ground; explorers leaping to shore to claim the wilderness for the Mother Country! Our collective sigh of relief seemed to echo across the glacier. Things would be easier for at least thirty yards. That's where the path met an even steeper snow field.

Rather than meet the slope head-on, we chose to crawl between the snow and rock wall which, while being safer, was much colder and more time consuming, and time was becoming a factor. We entered the claustrophobic passageway at 5:30. For two hours we scraped and scrunched at a glacial pace through the dark crawl space. In spots our packs would catch and wedge between the rock and ice while tiny rivulets of water spattered on our faces. When we exited the sun was much lower on the horizon. But the main obstacles seemed behind us. The next section of trail was a pure joy, more spectacular than anything we had ever experienced, but exhaustion dulled the enjoyment. We could not see the south summit and we really wanted to reach the cabin by dark.

We trudged happily up the trail which in many places had been dynamited from the rock. Our feet were aching, our shoulders sore and we were stopping frequently for water. But the thought of a relaxing night in the cabin on top of the world made the going easier.

The sun was beginning its evening descent into the cloud-covered lowlands when we reached the final snowfield. The snow was soft and the slope gentle. Roping up because we thought it was something climbers should do and would also look good on film, we marched up the snow and around a corner where we caught our first glimpse of the cabin. The lookout, seemingly plopped on top of the narrow rock pedestal beggared description. At that moment the Empire State Building or the Grand Coulee Dam made more sense. But it was to be our home for the night and we didn't waste much time contemplating the illogic of its position. We picked up the pace as much as our blistered feet would allow. As the sun set, we glanced over the east side of the mountain and and saw Glacier Peak suffused in the roseate afterglow of the sunset. Below us was nothing for a couple thousand feet. We held on tight.

One-hundred yards of trail carved into the side of the south peak brought us to a cleft almost completely blanketed in darkness. It was nearly vertical and looked unclimbable. There were three ladders which straddled and bridged the chimney but, unfortunately, they were almost rotten. In the gloom of oncoming darkness, with the wind whistling through, the narrow rock crevice awed us and we nervously debated the best approach. I didn't want to climb it. Craig said, "No way".

Jim, though, was eager and had disappeared into the shadows before we could question the wisdom of such a move. While he was stemming the chimney, I scrambled up a narrow scree slide to the left and peered down into the darkness of the Squire Creek Valley. That was not a practical route. Craig and I could only hear scraping and grunting in the depths of the chimney, but suddenly Jim reappeared forty feet above us, a silhouette poised to cross the chasm on a frail looking ladder with the middle rung missing. Craig looked at me and I looked at Jim, the ladder and the cabin, which now seemed more unapproachable and ghostly than it ever had from a distance. I yelled to Jim to come on down and, with great reluctance, he did. How could people clamber up these peaks? How could someone have spent his summers on that shaky perch? We weren't going to find out on this evening.

Without the cabin, we were in danger of becoming benighted without an appropriate campsite. The thought of bivouacking like the "Big Boys" of mountaineering never even entered our minds. We were not the Big Boys. I remembered passing a small platform on a heather slope just below the final snowfield. As darkness smothered us, we stumbled onto the small bench and collapsed; enough adventure for the day. The nook, obviously man made, sat next to a small stream and remnants of a cook stove were strewn about. Dinner was a simple affair; noodles and Spam washed down with grape Kool-Aid. Resting against our sleeping bags, we spent time star-gazing and marvelling at the lights of Snohomish, Everett, Seattle and beyond.

Craig had packed in a radio (the last time we were ever to take one with us in the mountains) and the voice of the DJ seemed to dance through the night sky from the city lights to our campsite in the meadow. We felt a comfortable isolation from the sea of civilization which surrounded us. The sights of the city and a friendly voice mixed with mountain sounds; a mild breeze, the splash of stream over rocks, the occasional high-pitched squawk of the gray jay. It was a strange and beautiful place. The lookout, many years ago, must have felt, at times, caught in a web, anchored on one side to civilization and wilderness on the other. He could see piers on the Seattle waterfront, watch cars travel along the streets of Darrington and almost step out his cabin door and touch them, almost. We lay in our sleeping bags, entranced by the spectacle of light, wondering if we could see the lights of our homes. What had our parents accomplished this day? They had gardened, shopped, swept and socialized, but they had not climbed a mountain. Well, neither had the three of us, but, as we lay in our sleeping bags, punchdrunk with exhaustion, we felt a little more like mountaineers.

The next morning we awoke to warm sunshine and a panorama of mountains I had never seen before. Emboldened by the sun we chose to return to Tin Can Gap via the lower slopes of the Three Fingers Glacier and found the going surprisingly easy. I snapped a picture of Craig leaping a crevasse that would surely impress the folks back home; never mind that it was only eighteen inches wide. At Goat Flats we stopped to wade in one of the ponds and look for goats. No goats. We stared at the cabin and wondered what a night on top might have been like. There seemed to be a lot about this mountain I wanted to know.

****

Since that first climb 17 years ago, I have returned to Three Fingers on numerous occasions: during heat waves, whiteouts, blizzards and monsoons. I laugh when I recall my terror on the snow slopes, but the scenery still takes my breath away. The only goat I ever saw on the mountain happened to wander out on the Three Fingers Glacier on the first day of goat hunting season; a score of eager-beaver hunters were combing Goat Flats for any sign of the nimble critters. We screamed at him to get the hell off the mountain.

I have slept in the cabin during storms so fierce I feared it would break free from the guy wires that held it earthbound. And I haved lazed against the cabin gazing at Puget Sound and the Straits of Juan de Fuca going blood red at sunset. Memories float around the mountain, but just as the pictures I took on the first trip, some are washed out and fuzzy while others remain pellucid, perfectly framed in the mind's eye.

I have also felt the presence of men and women who traveled the trail before me: people who built the cabin, those who manned the lookout and the climbers who have explored all the spires. What were George Vancouver's thoughts when he first sighted the mountain which must have served as a landmark for the expedition as its members mapped and named Puget Sound? Did the Indians of the Stillaguamish Valleys explore the mountain? The summit register only goes back to 1935, but I feel a kinship with people no longer alive, people I will never meet, who have hiked the trail that leads to the cabin or simply gazed longingly at this mountain which overlooks a fragile bit of wilderness on the edge of the tamed world.

Goat Flats in winter, late 1930's.

CHAPTER TWO

Evolution, Exploration, Exploitation

> ". . . and all behind me (and you) the ocean
> of tears which has been this life on earth,
> so old that when I look at panoramic
> photographs of the Desolation area and see
> the old mules and the wiry roans of 1935
> (Old Jack Mountain to an exact degree with
> the same snow arrangement) as they do in 1956
> so that the oldness of the earth strikes me
> recalling primordially that it was the same,
> they (the mountains) looked the same too in
> 584 B.C . . .

> — Jack Kerouac,
> Desolation Angels

If only the human mind could take it all in, the wrenching, rumbling march and retreat of geologic history. But as molecules on its immense timeline, we are rocked by the most insignificant geologic upheavals, an eruption, an earthquake, a small landslide. Like Kerouac, who spent a summer as a fire lookout on Desolation Peak, I have stared amazed at old pictures of Mt. Three Fingers. A forty-year-old picture of the mountain shows the Three Fingers glacier lacerated by scores of crevasses. The mountain looks so different to me. But what has actually changed? I can spot no perceptible differences in the three rock spires. Tin Can Gap, Whitehorse in the background, even the cabin look the same. What really jars me are the climbers standing at the Gap sporting ill-fitting rucksacks, knickers, pointy little caps and holding on to alpenstocks; how quaint, old-fashioned! My, how times have changed!

We punch in and out on the human time clock and our day is gone before we know it. Sitting in the meadows at Goat Flats or standing on top of the north peak or resting at Saddle Lake, I can for a short while, escape the inexorable grinding away of human time. For a second I can punch into geologic time.

The constancy of the mountain is comforting. Never mind that a million years ago Goat Flats was up to its tarns in glacial ice or that Three Fingers may have been a rounded rock dome. The mountain looks the same as it did seventeen years ago and

I imagine another seventeen years down the trail it will still look the same. Bob Dylan has sung "Time passes slowly up here in the mountains." That's fine by me.

****

Three Fingers and neighbors, Whitehorse, Bullon, Big Bear and Liberty, jut out from the main body of the North Cascades, their wooded foothills almost touching the backyards of town, suburb and city. Three Fingers, the centerpiece of this subrange, is ruggedly beautiful and familiar to the eyes of almost all who live in the Northern Puget Sound area, from Seattle to the Olympic Peninsula to Victoria, British Columbia. But ask a native to name it and you're likely to receive a shrug. "Let's see, Aunt Maude. Of course, you've got Rainier to the south. No mistaking that one. See that mountain to the north, the big white one that looks like a snowy molehill? That's Baker. It's volcanic, too. Shoot, I should know the names of those over to the east. One of them is Pilchuck. It used to have a ski area. It's closed. Not enough snow. But the others? Beats me. Aren't they something though? Bet you don't have hills like that in Topeka!"

Three Fingers, like most peaks in the North Cascades, is often lost in the considerable shadow cast by its volcanic brethren. It will never be mistaken for Rainier and no airline pilot will ever direct passengers to look out their windows in order to catch a glimpse of "majestic" Mount Three Fingers. But the mountain has its own special charms.

Bob Craig, who spent four summers in the Three Fingers lookout, commented, "Three Fingers always had several things going for it; a spectacular peak, in a small way, with a neat, small glacier. The mountain is not lost amongst the others on the crest. All life zones are nicely delineated. It is also one of the world's spectacular sunset spots and is identifiable from all directions."

Part of the mountain's allure lies in its past which is peopled with larger-than-life characters, rugged outdoorsmen who easily could have stepped out of Don Berry's novel *To Build A Ship* or Norman MacLean's *A River Runs Through It*. Men such as Harry Bedal, a modern day mountain man, tightlipped, strong and as comfortable living in the mountains as the animals he trapped and hunted. Harold Engles, a district ranger for the U.S. Forest Service who spent as much time hiking the hills and working the trails as the people he employed. John Lehman, an early Northwest mountaineer who was driven by his ambition to be the first man to climb Three Fingers. Harland Eastwood, who never let the loss of an arm keep him from becoming an accomplished mountaineer. Harry Tucker, whose childhood playgrounds were Whitehorse and Three Fingers. Before them are the stories of men who were convinced that the mountain contained unimagined mineral wealth and before those the earliest inhabitants of the surrounding river valleys, who believed the summit of Three Fingers to be the home of powerful spirits, both good and evil. And before man there was an even more amazing story.

When Harold Engles first considered putting a lookout cabin on the south finger, he knew it would present logistical problems; might even mean changing the look of the summit with a load of dynamite. But that seemingly dramatic facelift would be minuscule when compared with the changes which had already occured long before men began heading into the mountains and giving names to the land.

For millions of years the mountain had been caught in a violent geologic tug-of-war; push-pull, fold-stretch, freeze-fire, erode-erupt. The land was defined and redefined several times before it assumed a shape familiar to human eyes.

Past human knowing, the numbers become almost meaningless, but 500,000,000 years ago there was just water. Beneath this huge ocean was being laid the foundation for a mountain, made of marine sediments and volcanic rocks. Over the next 200,000,000 years a mountain range rose from the sea, but was eroded and in its wake was left sandstone, shale and conglomerates. The rock was folded and intruded by stronger granodiorites. Further chaos was wreaked on the land as magma pushed up through the surface and solidified leaving a massive, rounded plateau which stretched beyond the skyline. The intense heat of the volcanic rock hardened and recrystallized the rock which had been rudely displaced. Over time it became more resistant to the inevitable erosion which followed.

Six million years ago the mountain and its neighbors began to take on a familiar look. The cluster of peaks presented a bold and varied relief. The three gnarled and sharp rock fingers may have already begun their vigil looking over both mountain and lowland. A visitor to one of the summits might have seen another ocean, this time made of ice which had crept from the north and inundated all but the highest peaks. The visitor might have been able to scramble a few hundred feet to a notch between fingers and walk for days on the ice. The immense glacier probed to the heart of the range. Furrowing into the bedrock, the glaciers carved deep valleys, scoured the sides of mountains, leaving huge amphitheatres of polished slabs. These glaciers snaked around the three-fingered mountain and, 10,000 years ago when the ice retreated and eased its wintry grip on the land, rivers were left in their place, slowly loosening the mountain from its moorings to the main range.

The four seasons returned and the land turned lush and green. Forests of Douglas Fir, hemlock, cedar and spruce crowded mountain slopes and valley floors. Beneath their needled limbs flourished a profusion of huckleberrry, devil's club and fern. Stream banks were choked with vine maple and slide alder. Above timberline scrub pine shared wind-swept meadows with sunset colored wild flowers. And there was also rain.

Ocean storms, split by the mountain range to the west as they reached the coast, would meet again over the inland sound; and plow into the island of mountains. The three-fingered mountain might be veiled in drenching rain for days; numbed, soaked and nourished. Clouds would hang over the peak long after they had dissipated in the lowlands and around surrounding mountains. The large and small animals which lived on the mountains had heavy fur coats to protect them during the dark, wet days which made up a good portion of the year.

Into the wet, fertile land came the first human inhabitants, natives of Asia, who had crossed a land bridge in the Arctic which connected east and west. Those who eventually settled in the valley near the three fingered mountain called it Queest Alb. They used the rivers as trails. The rivers were good to them, providing an abundance of fish. The forests were alive with game animals. The mountains were not so kind and the Indians avoided the harsh land. A few men ventured into the hills to hunt the Sweet Lai (mountain goat). Its hair was used by the women to weave beautiful blankets. But the Indians rarely, if ever, climbed above timberline. To do so might anger the mountain spirits.

On a mountain near Queest Alb stood an eighty-foot rock face. Dwarf trees gave it curly hair. From the east, its weather-scarred face looked sinister, while from the west, it appeared more jovial. The Stolokwhamish (river people) were very cautious when hunting or berry picking near the crag and there were no campsites in the area.

The neighbors of the Stolokwhamish (Stillaguamish), who lived along the Sauk and Suiattle Rivers, traveled comfortably in the mountains and often crossed the range to trade with tribes to the east. Later they would guide white explorers through the rugged mountains.

The Stillaguamish had lived on the land for hundreds of years before they were visited by men from the east. The Spaniard, Manuel Quimper, sailed into the twenty-mile wide straits which bore the name of the first European to explore the waters, Juan de Fuca. Like Juan de Fuca, Quimper was in search of the elusive Northwest Passage. And like Juan de Fuca, he came away empty handed. During his expedition Quimper did make the first recorded sighting of Queest Alb. Two years later Captain George Vancouver, sailing under the British flag, brought his ship, the Discovery, into the sound and during his stay, poured names on the land like salt from a shaker. The names were rarely distinctive and often those of his crew.

During the spring of 1792, Vancouver and his men charted the inland sea that would soon bear the name of his lieutenant, Peter Puget. The weather, as noted in Vancouver's diary, was often fair and the men were treated to majestic views of "a very high, conspicuous craggy mountain . . . towering above the clouds . . . covered with snow and south of it was a long ridge of very rugged snowy mountains, much less elevated, which seemed to stretch a considerable distance."

In another entry, Vancouver wrote, "To describe the beauties of the region will, in some future occasion, be a very grateful task to the pen of a skillful panegyrist. The serenity of the climate, the innumerable pleasing landscapes and the abundant fertility that unassisted nature puts forth, requires only to be enriched by the industry of man with villages, mansions, cottages and other buildings, to render it the most lovely country that can be imagined."

In the center of the range was Queest Alb. From New Dungeness (Port Angeles) to New Georgia (Everett) to Hood Canal, the three fingers were visible to the Vancouver expedition. Queest Alb was never as effusively described as Baker or Rainier; a hidden blessing considering it could have been assigned the name of one of the crew. Mount Menzies? Mount Puget? Vancouver was, after all, charting the waters, not the interior.

Queest Alb would not be visited for another one-hundred years.

In the late 1800's men with dreams of becoming rich beyond caring began thrashing through the dense woodland undergrowth, wading mountain streams and crawling up rock faces in search of those telltale colors of copper, gold and silver. Fortune seekers came into the land of the Stillaguamish along with the first settlers. Before 1900 there were claims all over the slopes of So-bahli-ahli (Whitehorse) including one only 2,500 feet below the summit. In 1900 Charles and Pat Kelly set up a bornite claim at the head of Clear Creek, almost in the shadow of Queest Alb's 2,000-foot east face (men now called Queest Alb "Three Fingers"). Unlike most miners, who possessed little more than their grubstakes, the Kelly Brothers were backed by Eastern interests. A stake of $350,000 allowed the duo to start work on a huge tunnel and aerial tramway. Construction was finished by 1905 and there was a flurry of activity at the mine, but within four years the mine had closed. It was the same story all around Three Fingers and Whitehorse. No boom, mostly bust. A caretaker sat in a cabin at the bornite mine for ten years and in 1918 much of the equipment was disassembled. What was left rusted in the rain and disappeared under sword fern.

Joe Gerkman, a veteran of the Spanish-American War, had a hunch that deep in the small range of mountains one might find a bonanza. He placed a string of hunting camps up the Boulder River and tramped around the hills. Joe even did a little blasting just below Goat Flats. But he, too, was a caretaker, for an old timber mill on French Creek and most of his time was spent hunting, trapping and making friends with the animals that lived near his cabin. Keith Markwell who, in his youth, often visited Gerkman at his cabin, says, "Joe was an environmentalist fifty years before his time. Many times I saw him call wild rabbits out from the woods around his lower cabin. He could do it every time by calling 'Money, Money, Money'. Maybe he meant 'bunny', I don't know. He laboriously cleared out miles of trails around Mt. Bullon, 'so the goats can get around without scratching their wool off on the brush.' Gerkman always harbored dreams of striking it rich and jealously guarded his claims. But he never actively worked them."

By the early 1900's a crude dirt road connected the small community of Darrington with the outside world. A few Stillaguamish paddled the river and portaged from the North Fork to the Sauk, but many of the tribe, especially those living

Joe Gerkman.

Joe Gerkman's upper camp ("ooper coomp"), seven miles up Boulder River.

at Sauk Prairie, had been displaced by settlers and moved to land closer to the Sound or farther up the Suiattle River. The land around Three Fingers was owned by the Federal government and in 1905 the U.S. Forest Service was created to manage the forests. Fire trails were built to make easier access into the mountains. Hunters and the occasional hiker used these trails to get into the high country. Denny Pierson, from Arlington, made a few hunting trips around a mountain they called Sheepshank (Bullon). Ed Markwell first went into the Three Fingers area in 1914. He reached the saddle between Sheepshank and Three Fingers and found an old cedar goat snare, evidence that a few Indians had explored the alpine country beneath Three Fingers' dark, north face.

Keith Markwell says of his father, "Dad first considered it practical to take me into the Three Finger's area in 1929. The scenery was great and the trout fishing in Boulder Creek (I've not yet forgiven those who renamed it Boulder River) was unbelieveable; but it was the goats that captured my interest and they've never released it. Speaking of goats, until the late 1920's, Mt. Bullon was called Sheepshank. I've no idea why; there were never any sheep on it, nor does its shape suggest any such thing. Then the Forest Service submitted the name Mt. Bullon to honor Chan Bullin, a man who had been killed while working for the Forest Service in another area. Unfortunately, some bureaucrat blew it and spelled the poor man's name wrong and the mistake was never corrected."

Rare was the hiker, hunter, miner or Forest Service employee who was willing to battle the tangled underbrush without benefit of trails in order to reach Three Fingers. In 1927 Harold Engles moved to Darrington to assume the post of district ranger. The forests in his domain were huge, largely trackless. Thousands of acres were hidden from the few fire lookouts that served the district. Engles was struck by Three Fingers' distinctive spires and began mulling over the idea of constructing a lookout atop one of them. The energetic district ranger wanted to take a closer look at the mountain. In the fall of 1929, while visiting a trail crew near Tupso Pass, on Three Fingers' lower western flank, Engles decided the time was right for that closer look. Man was about to write his chapter in the mountain's history.

CHAPTER THREE

"Let's Go Take a Look at the Mountain"

It is late afternoon and I am wearily scraping my feet along the trail to White Pass, near Glacier Peak. I'm exhausted and have been the last four hours. At dawn, I started running from Stevens Pass, my goal Kennedy Hot Springs almost fifty miles to the north on the Pacific Crest Trail. But I have stopped running miles ago. The great undulation of the trail from valley to peak and back down again has left my legs oxygen-starved and rubbery. I have considered a bivouac at the pass, but friends have hiked into the hot springs to greet my "triumphant" arrival. I may let them down.

Before I reach the long, upward arcing slice of trail that leads to Red Pass, I meet two hikers. One man, older, sixty perhaps, greets me. He is tall and lanky, his sinewy arms impressively defined. His eyes, slightly squinted, give me a thorough going over, but his smile is friendly. He looks familiar. We chat and he is impressed with the miles I have covered.

"I hiked forty miles one day but never forty-seven", he says softly, shaking his head.

Hesitating, I finally ask, "Are you Harold Engles?" There are few men who would talk of forty-mile day hikes in such an offhanded manner. When he replies "Yes," I remind him of our first meeting seven years ago. "That's right, you came by with Dave Liming's son. Sure, sure. Funny meeting you here."

Harold and his hiking companion, Rick Maguire, give encouragement and bid me good traveling. Like me they have almost ten miles to cover that day.

Engles, on that day, was seventy-eight and still taking twenty-mile day hikes in the rugged Cascades. When I left the pass, I carried the picture of Engles, his shoulders only slightly touched by age, striding along the trail, Maguire following quickly behind.

Three years later we meet again, this time in his living room. It is difficult to discern any physical change. The voice is a bit softer perhaps, but there is no need for volume as the listener, captivated by stories of amazing men and amazing deeds, leans forward to catch every word. There is excitement in Harold's voice as if this were the first telling. He has a surprised laugh which punctuates anecdotes and, occasionally, his voice becomes even softer, conspiratorial, as if the subjects of his stories, Nels Skaar, Harry Bedal, Nels Bruseth, might be listening . . . "You know, Otto Sieb was a lookout for years on Pugh. Very particular. You put a cup on the wrong hook, he'd quietly remove it and put it on the right hook . . . I hiked up Pugh one day. There was a garden rake leaning against the wall. 'Who's gardening up here?' Nels Bruseth came out. He told me he used it for an ice axe . . . "

Engles worked with many "interesting" people. He hired many of them. But Harold was a boss who got out and worked side-by-side with trail crews, fire crews and lookouts. "We had an inspection outline that, theoretically at least, we were supposed to follow, but if you knew the fellow, you weren't going to do that. You were going to be friendly, work it out, the two of you. You couldn't be cold blooded. That's for the German Army, not me. The hell with that stuff. At Darrington we were all pretty close friends."

Many of those friends have been dead for many years, but Harold Engles doesn't live in the past. I gaze out the picture window which barely frames the broad, jagged summit of Whitehorse Mountain. The summit snowfield narrows and spills down the north slope almost all the way to Whiskey Gulch. There appears to be a line drawn along the peak's lower slopes where snow has turned to slush. Harold says, "I was up to Lone Tree Pass yesterday. The snow is waist deep in places."

Engles rises early every morning and hits the trail. In the winter when there is enough snow, he will strap on a pair of homemade cross country skis and glide for miles along the backroads. Each trip, no matter how brief, brings discovery, a new page in the book many would like him to write. For a man who has compressed the experience of three men into a lifetime, Engles still finds exciting possibilities in each new day. Leaning back in his chair, peering at, and beyond the wall to another time, past or future, he says, "Life shouldn't be worth a hoot when you get older. But it really gets more precious each day." There is a trace of amazement in his voice, the only hint one gets that Harold considers his extraordinary near-century of life as anything but ordinary, the way a man should live his life.

****

Harold Engles and Harry Bedal were awake before dawn

on September 25, 1929. The morning sky was slate gray and gloomy. The night before, Engles, the young district ranger in Darrington, had told Bedal, his trail foreman, "Let's go have a look at Three Fingers tomorrow." Harold wanted to build a fire lookout on the mountain's south summit. "The weather didn't look too good, but it was probably as good as it was going to get and I was closer to the mountain than I would be for quite a while."

The two men stuffed sandwiches into their canvas pants pockets, picked up a map, compass, aneroid and tramped off through the tangled climax forest which blankets the lower flanks of Three Fingers. The area was sketchily mapped and, as far as they knew, had never been explored. That fact deterred neither Harold nor Harry. Crashing through the brush was part of the job and, in their case, almost a specialty.

****

Harold Engles was born in 1902. At that time national forests were called forest reserves. In 1902 there were approximately 62,000,000 acres in reserve. The government body entrusted with their care was called the Bureau of Forestry; its clout was minimal. In May of 1903 the famed naturalist, John Muir, and President Theodore Roosevelt hiked through the Yosemite National Park, which was only ten years old. The two men talked candidly, on the trail and around backcountry campfires, about preservation of the wild lands of America.

In the late 1800's businessmen, entrepreneurs and politicians looked at America's vast western forests of Sequoia, Douglas Fir and Western Red Cedar, and saw dollar signs. Few saw an end to the seemingly endless bounty. Too few people championed the proposition that forest management must include conservation and preservation.

In 1897 Muir wrote in *The Atlantic*, "The American forests, however slighted by man, must surely have been a great delight to God; for they are the best he ever planted. The whole continent was a garden and from the beginning it seemed favored above all other wild parks and gardens of the world."

Muir bemoaned the coming of settlers to the continent who had in two hundred years stretched America's borders from ocean to ocean and had left in their wake "lands scorched into melancholy ruins." He concluded by saying, "Any fool can destroy trees. They cannot run away; and if they could, they would still be destroyed — chased and hunted down as long

Harold Engles on speeder car, Oakridge, Oregon. Harold had little trouble lifting the 150-pound hand car from track to track.

Harry Bedal in his prime.

as fun or a dollar could be got out of their bark hides, branching horns or magnificent bole backbones . . . God cannot save them from fools, only Uncle Sam can do that."

In Roosevelt, Muir found a sympathetic listener and powerful ally. Two years after their meeting, the young president in an address to the American Forestry Congress, urged lumbermen, miners and businessmen to look beyond self-interest, to "try to do his part toward seeing that our national policies are shaped for the advantage of our children and our children's children . . . Unless the forests of the United States can be made ready to meet the vast demands which this growth will inevitably bring, commercial disaster to the whole country is inevitable.

"If the present rate of forest destruction is allowed to continue, with nothing to offset it, a timber famine in the future is inevitable." The President cited devastation caused by fire, wasteful and destructive forms of lumbering and went on to outline a plan for a "national forest service" which would "make the national forests more actively and more permanently useful to the people of the West." Within a year, Roosevelt was able to put his plan into action. Gifford Pinchot, a longtime advocate of scientific management of forests, which included conservation and future growth, was selected by the President to head the Forest Service. In his autobiography, Pinchot remembered working quickly to create an organization which would "drive out red tape with intelligence and unite office and field . . . We could not adopt the methods of the Bureau (the previous, ineffective steward of the forest reserves) for both methods and results were thoroughly bad. We had no precedent that we could follow anywhere in the government service . . . We were indeed breaking new ground."

Pinchot welcomed suggestions for improvement, especially from men in the field in whom he put a great deal of trust. "When differences of opinion cropped up between field and office, as of course they did, it was my fixed intention to adopt the field men's recommendation unless there was strong reason against it. That was nothing more than strong horse sense."

From 1905 to 1909, National Forest land tripled, and the need for good men in the field grew apace. In 1918 Harold Engles, who twenty years later would hike with Gifford Pinchot in the Cascade Mountains near Mount Hood, became one of those "good men".

"I joined the Forest Service out of hunger, literally. My brother, who also went on to work for the Forest Service, a few friends and I were trying to make a go of living in a primitive and isolated cabin near Oak Ridge, Oregon. There were no roads to the cabin. We had to build a boat to get across the MacKenzie River to the nearest road, but we were young and brash and figured we'd make lots of money working in the woods. All our earnings went into a can stashed under a rock out back of the cabin. One day we decided to count it all and found $2. So much for the cabin. We needed food. I applied to the Forest Service, but I was too young, sixteen, and had to fake my age. The ranger asked and I told him twenty-one. Later on I had to do some fancy changing. I worked in the Cascade National Forest which is now the Willamette. I hadn't gone to college and I realized that if I wanted to move up I would need a little more education. So I took a special course. That was about sixty years ago. At the time I was the equivalent to an assistant ranger.

"I moved to Darrington in 1927. I'm not sure I was too enthused about the move. I wrote to my supervisor and told him that he was in a better position to judge. I was young, but as the district Ranger in Darrington I had lots of responsibilities, lots of timber sales. I can recall my first day in Darrington. It was a cold, clear day and the peaks stood out beautifully. The memory stands out clearly because I was about to start out on a larger, more active district. Being young, the thought never occurred that I might sit down and write about it almost sixty years later."

Engles inherited one full-time employee in Darrington. That man was in charge of timber sales and Harold was in charge of the rest. He worked out of a small, unfinished building on the north end of town. There was no electricity. Engles was ranger, timber cruiser, blacksmith and secretary. The District had at its disposal a railroad speeder car, a few oxen and horses. The Forest Service insisted that the new district ranger buy his own truck which Engles did eventually, a Dodge Roadster, with a truck bed added. "At the time the Forest Service couldn't afford trucks, but they did give me mileage. I traveled by horse more often than not.

"We had lookouts on Pugh and Higgins, with secondary cabins in places like Glacier Ridge, Whitechuck Flats, French Creek and Red Mountain. So much of our time back then was spent traveling, but that's what I enjoyed."

The twenty-five-year-old Engles was the perfect hiking machine. He stood well over six feet, carried not an ounce of fat on his lean, muscular frame and had the constitution to match. Engles, a victim of the great influenza epidemic of 1919, had lain in bed unconscious for three days. But he recovered from the killer which claimed over a half-million lives in the United States.

One had to be prepared to hike in high gear when he hit the trail with Harold. Harold had legs and lungs that never quit. One morning, after scaling logs down at Swede Heaven, which sits in the shadow of Mount Higgins, he decided to climb up and over the 5,500 foot peak and visit the lookout along the way. Higgins' long ridge is ragged, steep and trailless, a serious alpine traverse. Engles, wearing tennis shoes, managed the ten-mile traverse to the lookout in a little less than eight hours. "I sure surprised the lookout when I came in the back door."

A big part of Engles' job was determining where to build trails. "One summer we built seventy-nine miles of horse trails. The men who worked on the trails were hard working, competent and dedicated. You couldn't have built the lookout on Three Fingers without men like that. After fifty years I can still locate trails that have long been abandoned. I have to stop a moment and think, 'Where did we put it in?', but I find them. Today the Forest Service contracts out the trail building and very few new trails are being built.

"Fires were a problem and the trails were necessary to reach the valleys and high country. We had lots of private logging going on in the Stillaguamish Valley and there would be quite a bit of slash, farmers clearing the land. The first year I came here, we had a 6,000-acre fire, lightning caused. In 1927 we took in the Silverton District to the south which made the trails more important because there were so few roads. There were four or five ways to get across the mountains to Silverton. I spent most of my time hiking those trails and I usually took a Pulaski to make improvements on the trail (a Pulaski is a long-handled trail-building tool, half hoe and half pick). The farther out you got, the worse the trail. I'd also take a pair of pliers to fix broken telephone lines. The Forest Service was pushing for, what they called, "Progressive Travel". If you were someplace, get some work done rather than making lots of trips. At that time, while I was out on the trails, I was reading Voltaire's *Letters on The*

English. When they were published, he had to flee from France immediately because they were quite an expose on the government. On his way out of the country, he snapped up another man's wife and took her with him. Evidently Progressive Travel was nothing new. I wrote a little article about Voltaire and Progressive Travel for our bulletin, but the office wouldn't print it. I didn't sign it either.

"With the larger territory, I determined we needed better fire protection. I was from Oregon where there was more fire hazard and I was still in the mood to expect fires everywhere. I got around to all the lookouts that first year and it just looked to me that we weren't covering enough area. The more I saw places like Three Fingers, the more I thought we should take a look at them. I must have climbed a half-dozen or more peaks. Harry and I even took a look on Sloan Peak, but it was too tough and Mt. Pugh covered most of that area anyway. Three Fingers seemed practical, though. It was visible from so many places. You hike up Squire Creek, which is quite a watershed and there's Three Fingers. Three Fingers commanded a view of Upper Clear Creek and even into the South Fork of the Stillaguamish. I spotted the mountain from so many places and it seemed to eliminate a lot of blind spots in our detection system.

"In the fall of 'Twenty-nine, Harry Bedal's crew was building a trail from the Boulder up to Tupso Pass to connect with a trail coming up the South Fork of Canyon Creek. I came up to take a look and that evening I told him I thought it would be a good idea if we hiked up and took a look at Three Fingers. He replied, 'Yes'. Harry was never one to waste words but there was no better partner in the mountains. He started working for the Forest Service the same year I did. I spotted Harry and Nels Skaar and thought, 'These two should be working for the Forest Service.'

"Nels was quite a character. He had immigrated from Norway and still had problems with his R's and J's. He had worked for Jim Bedal, Harry's dad, cutting shingle bolts. One time he called Jim from Seattle and said, 'Yim, I'm in Yail. Send me fifty dollars.' Another time he hired a taxi to get him from Seattle to Darrington. He only made four dollars a day. One winter he read the dictionary from cover to cover. Nels ran a trail crew for me, an excellent woodsman.

"One summer his crew was camped at the head of Crystal

Creek and between the bunch of them, they had a guitar, harmonica, jew's harp and fiddle. In the evenings they'd get on the radio and perform. It could be heard at the main office and at some of our residences, besides the lookouts. At the office, it came in over what we called a 'Howler'. Nels would get on the line and announce, 'The Cwystal Cweek Okastwah is on the air. For our first number we'd like to play . . .' Well, the title was a bit bawdy and it came into the office loud and clear. He didn't know it, I'm sure. But I got on the line the next day and said, 'Nels, you start with another opening number. Forget you ever heard the other one.' It's funny now, but it was embarrassing at the time. I can tell you that song is responsible for the naming of Rat Trap Pass. Nels was quite the optimist. His expression for even the worst situations was 'Splendid'. He'd look at huge rocks blocking the way and exclaim, 'Splendid'. He really gave people a lift.

"Harry Bedal was already a legend when I came to Darrington. He was born at Sauk Prairie in 1890 and the next year the family moved to their homestead several miles up the Sauk River. You could only reach it by trail. His mother was the daughter of a Suiattle Chief who had guided the Northern Pacific surveyor over the Cascades in 1870.

"Harry's sisters, Jean and Edith, who are still alive and active, learned to make coiled baskets from cedar roots and weave blankets from mountain goat wool. My wife, Anna May, has some baskets made by the Bedal sisters. They are beautiful and well made. Jim Bedal taught his children outdoor skills early. He'd done about anything you can think of in the mountains, even worked in the mines at Monte Cristo. By the time he was five or six, Harry was using a hammer and a piece of drill steel and drilling holes through the rocks on the river bar near his home. He was also falling trees, but his father put a stop to that.

"Harry loved the challenge of the mountains. He loved to take the hard way. He was an expert marksman, canoer, shingle bolt cutter. He spent weeks alone in the mountains building camps and trapping. He was also a good cook. His hot cakes were great. Harry guided and one fall he hoisted an injured hunter on his back and carried the guy for several miles without stopping. Harry wasn't tall, about 5-10, but he was powerfully built. He had big shoulders and was strong from the toes up. He weighed about 205 pounds but there was no fat. When he went into the army during World War I, he passed the physical perfectly, not even a cavity; the only one in the state of Washington. Harry was something for the doctors to study.

"Harry knew this area better than anyone. I recall we were locating trail near Falls Creek. We'd been making our way through thick timber for quite a ways when Harry stopped, took a stick, bent over and cleared away moss and sticks. Underneath he found some wood ashes from an old campfire. He told me he'd camped here with a party of Indians thirty-seven years ago when he was seven! That was Harry. He noticed things that never register with most people. He had good instinctive judgement. I had to rely on maps, a compass, all that stuff because I wasn't as much a hillbilly as he was. Both Harry and Nels were truly at home in the woods, but you know, both of them ended up in the city. Nels moved to Seattle in the 'Thirties and was repairing skis. He tripped on a curb, had a heart attack. People ignored him. They mistook his condition for intoxication and he died. Harry got married and moved to San Francisco to work in the shipyards during World War II. He was a young man, only 55, when he died in 1945. I don't think a man like Harry should ever get around a city. Those city germs are no good. We're not immune to them. I always claimed, and I know Edith and Jean Bedal agree, that you couldn't have gotten Harry Bedal with anything else."

****

"Harry and I left before the trail crew awoke. They didn't give our little trip a second thought. We were always heading off into the woods like that. We didn't get back to the crew for a couple of days, but they didn't worry. In those days, if you didn't show up, they scratched your name off the list. It was so different. When Harry and I left the trail camp at Tupso Pass that morning, we had a general idea of where we wanted to go. We had sketched, what we called, a seen and unseen map. It was very basic but we hit Saddle Lake, then unnamed, without a hitch. It was a control point. I figured from the lake we could hit the ridge which appeared on the contour map. We pretty much stayed on that ridge. A ways above Saddle Lake, just as we were getting out into the open, we ran into a prospector's hole. It turned out that Joe Gerkman had been up there and dynamited the hole. I talked to him about it and he told me to get out of there because it was his territory. He meant it too. Joe once wrote the president because the government put a trail across his trapline. Oh, he was touchy about such things!

"Joe had worked at the Standard Railway and Timber Company as a timber faller and when it closed, the company left him there, about three miles up the French Creek Road, as watchman. After a while there was nothing much left to watch. He just got in the habit. He trapped and had a camp way up the Boulder River where the forks meet. But Joe really survived on his pension from the Spanish-American War. Joe would come into town when he'd get his check and say, 'Set em up'. He'd get his beard trimmed, the whole works, then he'd head back to French Creek. Joe was all right. I cultivated his friendship, brought him things, and we got to be pretty good friends.

"Joe fancied himself a pretty fair cook and he'd always offer you his stew and homemade wine. One Friday the wife of one of our trail crew drove up the road to pick up her husband at the trailhead. There was Joe standing next to his cabin. When she stopped he offered her some of his stew, but she told him she had to hurry. When she returned, Joe was standing in the middle of the road with a spoon and kettle. As she rolled down the window to tell him they couldn't stay, he shot a spoonful of stew into her open mouth. Joe stayed in his cabin until 1950 when his arthritis got so bad they had to take him to the Veteran's hospital in Seattle where he died shortly thereafter.

"The trail to the lookout goes right by Joe's hole in the ground. You know, an awful lot of the time we were pretty much where the trail is today. That was one of our goals. When we reached Goat Flats, we got a chance to look around and see some peaks. We stayed on that ridge above the Flats until cliffs forced us down near, what I call, Saddle Camp. They changed the name to Tin Can Gap after I left in 1937. I wasn't too happy about that. From the Gap, we worked our way across the ridge to the top of Three Fingers, well, pretty close. The summit of the South Finger is split, and we squeezed up that chimney until all we had to do was make a long step across. It was wet out and the rock had an inch of snow on it. You didn't want to miss. I stood looking at the other side for five minutes trying to figure out whether to jump or not. I finally decided to wait for another day. I don't know whether I would have made it or not and with the snow on it, well . . .

"Harry and I wanted to use the map I'd made, but we couldn't see so we decided to head down. It wasn't storming but it was raining and we thought we'd try to get down into Squire Creek rather than back-tracking. A break in the clouds

Harold Engles, 81, packs in to Goat Flats.

Engles in late 1920's.

gave us a view but we still had to do a bit of careful shooting with the compass. The ridge down to the gap between Three Fingers and Big Bear Mountain is fairly steep. At the gap we met a bear. We used to see them all the time. You don't anymore. Too many are getting shot. The two of us slid down a chimney and headed over to Squire Creek Pass. It got dark as we were heading down the trail and we got off into the brush. We had one candle and Harry carried it. He would get out ahead of me and I'd be fighting the brush, but Harry would keep going. Eventually we ended up wading down the middle of Squire Creek. We got dunked a couple of times. It was slippery and we really got soaked. I've hiked with some pretty tough hikers before, but heck, they didn't know they were tough and I didn't either. Harry, in a very quiet way, was as tough as they come. I can't ever imagine him getting tired. He was strong and had lots of endurance, but he never pushed himself. There's no telling what he could have done if he had tried.

"The two of us finally arrived in Darrington about 11 p.m. Harry lived in the hotel and I hiked back to the ranger station. The next morning we took big packs and hiked up to meet the trail crew. Certainly surprised them. Yes, that was quite a day.

"To me it's a bit of a dream. But at the time we didn't think anything of it. It was just a day's work. I'm not a mountain climber, never pretended to be. I like the mountains real well, but Harry and I didn't think about climbing a mountain. We were thinking, 'Can we get a lookout up here?' Years later I discovered this mountain climbing is quite a business. I sometimes think about climbing Three Fingers that day. It was over nineteen miles on no trails, and I say to myself, 'That son-of-a-gun was one tough son-of-a-gun.'

"After looking at the summit, Harry and I figured we could build a lookout. It wasn't going to be easy, but the office was ready to trust my judgement. I'd had a little trouble because I was young. I thought it would be like Pugh, but it was worse. We decided to go ahead with it anyway. Heck, I didn't have any brains. At that age you've got energy and you're not supposed to have any brains. Youth takes the place of brains. Youth can do anything. Harry and I talked it over and we knew there were lots of men who'd be glad to tackle something like Three Fingers. There was a certain amount of romance and we knew those young men would extend themselves. On Three Fingers they'd have to."

CHAPTER FOUR

"I Never Hired Out to be No Eagle"

A curious calm settles over the Stillaguamish Valley before dusk. Gusts fade to whispers. The leaden cloud cover breaks on the horizon and sun, streaming through the creases, turns the sky a brilliant amber. It is a good time for reflection and remembrance. On this particular afternoon, Harold Engles has invited Edith and Jean Bedal to his home. With these two Darrington pioneers, conversation turns easily to stories of the past. Many of the reminiscences are punctuated by, "I remember that so clearly" or simply a knowing smile. Feeling all-too firmly rooted in the present, I am content to sit back and let each story take me back three-quarters of a century; the historical hitchhiker.

Their father, Jim Bedal, an early pioneer in the Sauk valley, had left the family farm in Illinois at age 20, worked on Mississippi river boats for a while and eventually drifted west to Washington where he found work at the Skagit Queen mine. In 1889 he made his way to Sauk Prairie, home of the Sauk tribe and he became acquainted with the chief, Wawakum. Jim liked the man and he liked his daughter, Suzanna. Wawakum gave Bedal permission to ask for his daughter's hand in marriage and she accepted.

Bedal eventually homesteaded fifteen miles up the Sauk River. A horse trail or difficult canoe paddle was the only connection with Darrington. Jean and Edith were both born at the Bedal homestead. Theirs was truly a pioneer life, rustic and rigorous. For many years the girls were educated at home. Along with their brother, Harry, the women learned how to survive in the wilderness and developed an affinity for its wildness. The mountains became their spiritual as well as physical home. Jean has written of their life at Bedal: "It was like living in the hollow of the cupped hand of God."

I have looked forward to meeting the Bedals for some time and hope to gain some insight into the personality of their illustrious brother, Harry. Harold's silent partner seems to hover over my enterprise, a shimmering mirage which tantalizes just beyond one's grasp. I would love to summon Harry Bedal from the past for a conversation, but I suspect he would probably let his close friends do most of the talking. Jean and Edith have collected several scrapbooks worth of pictures and clippings. There are pictures of Harry in uniform during World War I, as a member of the tribal canoe team, working the family asbestos claim high on the slopes of Sloan Peak, driving shingle bolts down the Sauk River and building the Three Fingers lookout cabin. The photographs and anecdotes reinforce the image in my mind of a strong, silent and very private man. I sense that Harry was a bit of an enigma even to those who knew him best. But to have known him at all was, for Harold, more than enough.

Jean and Edith share many of their brother's qualities. They are quiet, energetic and adventuresome. But there are differences. Harry enjoyed a joke, but his was a muted laugh. According to Harold, Harry's shoulders would shake and a slight smile would form on his lips. The Bedal sisters possess hearty and infectious laughs and both Jean and Edith take delight in poking gentle fun at Harold. Neither sister is as stingy with words as was Harry and both write. Jean is working on a tribal history and a few years ago Edith began writing about her early life at Bedal. Encouraged by Jean and Harold, she reads one of her stories.

"I broke my ankle while hiking on the Pacific Crest Trail south of Rainy Pass (she was 79). While convalescing, I had time on my hands and decided to write."

A clock sitting on the mantle ticks softly, soothingly, a quiet metronome measuring the lyrical cadences of Edith's voice, which assumes an adolescent innocence as she describes life at the Bedal home seventy years ago.

"It was a hot, hot day in August (1918). Mother and I had climbed through dry, forestless terrain (on Sloan Peak), which was steep and without brush . . .

"At a cliff Mother dropped her pack and I did likewise. She said, 'We'll have to tie our packs with rope and haul them over the rocks one at a time' . . . After the packs were over the cliff, I climbed around and joined Mother. There were no more rock formations as we continued climbing the forest slopes. Eventually the trees became smaller as we neared the top. It was sundown as we reached the highest point. Small hemlocks and open glades made a pretty panorama. We were on the ridge extending from Sloan Peak . . . It was surprising to see Mt.

Pugh looming against the evening sky, so close. Mother look-ed at me and said, 'We came up the wrong creek. Father gave us the wrong start. We should have followed the other creek below the Penn Mine (at Goat Lake).'

"Once oriented we were ready to camp for the night. We found a level spot between trees and bedded down. The sum-mer night was balmy and we slept well in our bed of two blankets, one to lie on and one on the top for covering . . . In the morning we reached Father's old camp which he had nam-ed Bean Camp."

The Bedal children became adept woodsmen at an early age. There was no such thing as "A woman's place . . . ", although when I point to a picture of women climbing Glacier Peak in dresses, Jean laughs and exclaims, "Oh goodness yes, you couldn't wear P-A-N-T-S then. It was a different age." Such social customs were of little importance at the Bedal home, in the woods, on the trails guiding hunters, along the traplines or at the asbestos claim, the Phoenix, high on Sloan Peak.

" . . . Father wanted us to collect asbestos samples from a formation he had discovered in his younger years. He was disabled by a stroke. It was a time of great depression and Father thought he could make some money although the asbestos mine was located in a most inaccessible region.

"Harry had made some cash horse packing and fur trap-ping, but even the fur market was at a low ebb. By living off the land at the Bedal place, we were able to weather hard times. That July, there was no money. Previously there had been money while Father was in the shingle business and Mother would take us to town to see the sights. She said, 'We can't stay home on the 4th. Let's do something different. Let's climb Sloan Moun-tain. Harry, Jean and I agreed. It was a beautiful time although at my age I had not yet been completely captivated by the wilderness and I missed the excitement of the 4th and the crowds of young people. Harry was the only one who had real fun glissading. Jean and I were too timid to try snow skiing, but it was a change from the hum-drum life at Bedal.

"The next year Father decided Harry should do some ex-ploration work at the asbestos site. The mine never panned out, but Harry built a trail to the mine and later a cabin. On these trips Harry took a little kitten with him, a true companion."

Jean explains that Harry would come home for the weekends. One weekend he found a new litter of kittens. He placed one

Edith Bedal, left, and Jean Bedal Fish, 1983.

Edith Bedal with pack horse, White Pass, 1929.

The Harry Bedal home, 1929.

in the pocket of his mackinaw jacket and took him back to the cabin. By the end of the summer, Harry and the kitten were good friends. It was quite a sight to see Harry riding his horse up the trail with the kitten following close behind.

"Harry built the cabin of natural, peeled logs, split cedar boards. It had cedar tables, a front porch and picture window. It was the perfect mountain dwelling. It became a home for us. The horses had plenty of forage and would wander up steep slopes like goats."

Jean and Edith's attachment to the mountains grew during those summers spent at Harry's cabin. Edith continues her reading: "I learned the skills of high altitude climbing and I loved every moment of it. One afternoon Mother decided to go goat hunting. We climbed up steep shale slopes. We didn't see any goats, no fresh steaks for dinner, but I enjoyed the challenge."

One summer, while still in high school, the two girls took parties into the mountains to earn "some pin money." For a time Edith trapped for furs. She had a trap line that ran to Harry's cabin. She remembers carrying a small pack, containing, among other things, a small, hand-made candle lantern and a Colt 45. Over her shoulder she slung a pair of snowshoes. One wintry afternoon Edith reached the cabin, only to find it covered with snow. She had to dig furiously to reach the door and spent the night waiting out a great blizzard.

" . . . The years passed quickly. The longer I lived up river, the enchantment with the beautiful country grew. The valley and high mountains were my home. When World War II arrived, I was still living at the homestead with Mother. It was getting overgrown and Harry's cabin had not been used for several years. With great nostalgia I would think of the wonderful sojourns we had in our cabin in the sky at Sloan Peak. Several years later I returned to the cabin. The trail was overgrown. We hacked away with hatchets and had to wade Bedal Creek. There was nothing left of the cabin. A snow slide had destroyed it. Nature had relentlessly claimed its own, but my memories are still vivid."

Harold, who has lately hiked around the old Bedal homestead, remarks on the crop of head-high nettles he found. "It's good, rich land", he says and adds, "It's a good thing we have memories."

After spending several years in the Seattle area, Jean and

Edith resettled closer to the mountains, Edith in Darrington and Jean in Arlington. Jean served as chairman of the Sauk-Suiattle Tribe and was a driving force in the tribe's successful bid for reservation status. She is currently working on a history of the tribe, in part to preserve the history, and also literally to keep the tribe and its heritage alive. In her history of the Sauk-Suiattle she writes, "The rugged mountains, the lonely valleys, the long accustomed hunting grounds, all now know them no more. Today this once proud race remain little else than strays or waifs upon the tides of time." Edith, in addition to her writing has been doing Vista volunteer work and also works for the tribe.

In 1982, shortly before her accident, Edith hiked to Goat Flats. She first visited the mountain in 1936 when Harland and Catherine Eastwood were manning the lookout. Despite the injury, Edith remains optimistic about hiking in the mountains again, perhaps finishing her traverse of Washington's Crest Trail. To one who loves them, dreams of the mountains die hard. A cane rests next to Edith and it is difficult to imagine her returning to the mountains, but her face, while weathered like her sister's, is only slightly touched by the years. Her arms are strong and so is her will. Jean still gets out in the hills. I suspect Edith also will return to the mountains.

I am surprised when Anna Mae Engles invites us to the dinner table. It is dark out and I hadn't noticed. I look at my notebook and realize how many notes I have taken. It has been quite a trip, one that I really didn't want to end. Noticing my bemused expression, Harold laughs and says, "You're getting a world of history today. It sort of jolted you. I thought it would."

****

September 24, 1931 was a perfect fall day and Jim Tucker wasn't about to waste it. He was busily at work in the backyard of the Tucker homestead at the base of Whitehorse when the afternoon calm was shattered by an explosion. The younger Tucker children scurried for cover, but the blast had ocurred at least three mountains to the south on Three Fingers. The mysterious explosion, set by Harry Bedal and his Forest Service trail crew, had flattened the summit of the south peak, spraying the air with dust and huge chunks of rock. In Darrington Harold Engles and Nels Bruseth stepped outside the Forest Service office to listen for the explosion. The crew had sent word that the blasting would commence that afternoon.

The two rangers heard an indistinct rumble in the distance, but they weren't sure. What Engles could be sure of was that, after two years of building trail and hauling materials, his plan to put a lookout cabin on top of Three Fingers was about to become more than possibility.

Despite wet snow and swirling clouds which had obscured the view, Engles and Harry Bedal had returned from their epic one-day reconnaissance of the mountain convinced that a cabin could be constructed on the south peak. They also knew it would not be an easy task, but the Seattle office of the Snoqualmie National Forest (the Darrington Ranger District wasn't transferred to the Mount Baker Forest until 1933) approved Engles's proposal. By June of 1930 he was ready to go.

"We had been putting in trails on Meadow Mountain and down into Canyon Creek. There was also a plan to build a recreational horse trail to Goat Flats whether or not the lookout was approved. The people who owned the Canyon Creek Lodge wanted to build a hunting lodge at Goat Flats. The Depression put an end to that scheme. We spent most of the summer on those other trails, but on Three Fingers we got the trail as far as Goat Flats. On August 14, Harry and I climbed the south peak to take a look around. This time the weather was better and we took the step across to the summit. We also blasted rock until late in the evening. The detonator was not working well. We used to prepare shots for blasting after the crew had left for camp, a safer practice and made for less time on the job.

Dynamite can make a person jumpy. One day, I recall during World War II, I hiked up the Mt. Pugh trail to set a small charge to remove a rock in the trail, about a mile below the cabin. As I was approaching the cabin, the two lookouts came running down the trail. I asked them what was the matter and they yelled, 'The mountain blew up!'

"The next day on Three Fingers, Harry and I located the trail to Tin Can Gap and studied the steep rock ridge that cut across the trail. There were going to be some tricky spots on the new trail. A month later Harry and I brought Louis Treen, the deputy supervisor in charge of construction, up to the south peak. I scrambled up without a rope and he thought I had a lot of nerve, but he said, 'If you want to try it (building the lookout), it's okay with me.' The next summer I accompanied Superintendent William Weigal on a climb of the mountain. We got caught in a dirty, little electrical storm, but he was impressed with the site. He was 65 and wanted to prove his fitness by climbing to all the lookouts in the district. He did it too.

"I wasn't able to spend as much time on the Three Finger project as I would have liked in 1931. At the time we had a very extensive trail construction program and the time I could spend at any one project was limited. I was also supervising the Civilian Conservation Corps, the CCC's. We had two hundred men in each camp; the mayor of Everett, Bill Moore, was a CCC. There was also the ERA, made up of mostly local men, older. I even had a straight Indian ERA crew. I had more latitude with the ERA boys because we could send them out overnight. The young men in the CCC's had to be back to camp every evening. They built other lookouts but were not involved with Three Fingers. Most trails at the time cost $50-$100 a mile, but Three Fingers was going to be more expensive, about $300 a mile. None of the trail was easy, even the section from Tupso Pass to Saddle Lake. That climax forest is a mess, tangled hemlock roots, choked and wet. I had seven crews besides the group on Three Fingers and you spend the most time where you're needed the most. With Harry running things on Three Fingers, I could afford to concentrate on the other business."

Albert "Curly" Towne, along with his brother, Ed, Tom Ash, Curly Peterson, Ralph Daniels and Fred Fuller, were members of the six-man trail crew. Albert remembers the experience clearly. Like many men in the early 1930's, he was thankful for whatever work came along and he took the job the Forest Service offered without hesitation. A job was a job no matter where it might take him.

While packing supplies needed for their summer on the mountain, Towne became acquainted, not only with his co-workers, but with the mules in Cactus Robinson's string. Wild Fire and Dynamite, as their names suggested, possessed explosive tempers. Wild Fire had once autographed the eight-foot ceiling of the stable with his hindfoot prints. Dynamite was prone to violent temper tantrums but was also devious. A favorite trick was to take a deep breath while the pack strap was being tightened. He would then relax and the pack would slide off. At other times he would take a more direct approach; bucking and braying until the pesky load was dumped on the ground.

After packing summer gear, the crew battled their way up a trail overgrown with huckleberry and littered with blowdowns.

Left to right, the legendary Harry Bedal; Frank Benesche, carpenter; and Tom Ashe, at the last camp on the Three Fingers trail.

Above the last camp, Gerald Ashe leads the pack string
with Elwin Robinson, packer, riding.

Dynamited summit before lookout construction. Left to right, Curly Peterson; unidentified; Gerald Ashe.

Ed Towne operates windlass, hoisting materials to the summit in 1931.

Curly Peterson, left, and Gerald Ashe on Three Fingers
trail above last camp, 1931.

Left to right, Harold Engles and Harry Bedal on Mt. Pugh trail
during period of lookout construction in 1927.

Swarms of huge mosquitoes, looking for blood donors, tormented the men, who masked themselves with cloth soaked in citronella. It seemed to repel the pesky mosquitoes, but Towne almost preferred the bugs to the aromatic citronella.

The hard days on the trail were lightened by humor. One of the younger members of the crew, spotting a small hill of what he assumed was coal, ran toward it shouting that he had struck it rich. His potential bonanza of black gold, on closer inspection, turned out to be freshly deposited bear scat. The crew bestowed the name Bear Cove on the spot that day and nicknamed poor Chester, "Stinky".

The court jester of the crew was Ralph Daniels, whose moniker was "Tennessee". Towne considered him to be the funniest man he ever met, a comedian who could have reduced the crew to wild giggling with the announcement of his impending death. Like all good comedians, Daniels had a superb sense of timing and a punchline, delivered in his rich Southern drawl, invariably produced riotous laughter from the rest of the crew and that really helped because the men went through a great deal of hardship building that trail.

You needed men like Ralph because they made the work easier. It would have been good business to hire a man for the crew whose only job would have been to keep the men laughing, keep their spirits up," Harold Engles said.

The crew spent most of the summer drilling and dynamiting the rock which blocked the path of the proposed trail above Goat Flats. Trails were carved in the steep snow slopes above Tin Can Gap and covered with gravel so that mules could reach the final camp several hundred feet below the peak. The mules packed in a forge fueled by blacksmith coal. Engles remembers, "We were doing so much drilling that we were constantly sharpening. Fred Fuller's job was to sharpen the steel. All the drilling was done by hand, double jacking, with one man hammering while another held and turned the drill. Often we had to drill holes four or five feet into the rock. We must have used at least nine cases of dynamite on Three Fingers.

"In September, when we were ready to blast on the summit, I packed in a load of dynamite. One of the pack horses fell into the Boulder River. I jumped in and held her head out of the water while we unhitched her pack. We lost time saving the dynamite and the horse, but one blast pretty much got the job done. We pretty much leveled the top with one blast, although there were many irregular, jagged spots left, which required quite a bit of trimming. We used a single jack for the drilling and it usually took about an hour to drill a four-to-five foot hole. One man had to spoon out the dust accumulating in the hole otherwise the drilling would have been impossible. Today men use power jacks and it's kind of pathetic to think of all the time it used to take us to drill by hand.

"The men spent a lot of time chipping away at cracked rock to get as flat a surface as possible. You'd grab a sledgehammer and whang away until you'd gotten rid of the loose rock. With all the loose rock flying through the air we should have been wearing goggles but we didn't. We didn't have them. Harry and the crew did a great deal of blasting on top, but they had had to be careful that they didn't shoot off too much of the platform. There wasn't any to waste."

From the final camp below the summit, the materials for the cabin were winched to the top. Ed Towne, who had worked on the Mt. Pugh trail, remembers working the windlass on top. "As I wound it, my body leaned out over a vertical drop of a thousand feet. I tried to keep most of my body over solid ground, but I still didn't like the feeling. If the wire holding the windlass had ever broken, you would have flown out into space. Generally a load would consist of two bundles of planks and we could winch them up in a couple of minutes. The dynamiting was pretty exciting too. I swear, one time we hid under a big boulder during a blast and some of the rocks that whizzed by were larger than the boulder.

"One day I was sent to Tin Can Gap to get more dynamite. As I was carrying the load up the ladders to the summit, I kept hearing an odd sound and asking myself, 'What's that noise?' Tom Ash replied that it was a swarm of bees. It sounded like the humming of a Model T coil. I knew something was wrong and so did Harry Bedal. He took off his hat and his hair was standing on end. An electrical storm was imminent.

"Harry told me to take off my hat. My hair stood on end. He scratched his head and said, 'We better get out of here.' Considering the amount of dynamite I was carrying, that was an understatement."

Neither Ed nor Albert got used to the dizzying heights. Albert recalled, on his first trip to the future site of the cabin, being almost paralyzed after peering over the edge. With a great deal of effort, he was able to compose himself, but he has never quite gotten over his fear of heights. During the Depression, one couldn't afford the luxury of leaving a job because of acrophobia.

One day Ed Towne and Tom Ash were drilling a hole on the flattened summit. Ash was holding the bit and had to sit with one leg dangling over the edge of the cliff while Ed drilled. "Tom asked me if I wanted to change places. I hastily replied that I felt fine right where I was. When I first stood on top, I told Harry Bedal, 'I ain't no eagle and I never hired out to be no eagle.'"

While the trail crew was constructing the last stretches of trail, a two-man crew was stringing the telephone wire from Tupso Pass to the summit. According to Harold Engles, "Keeping the line up was quite a chore. The coiled steel was strong enough, although it only had a tensile strength of 650 pounds, compared to 1800 for the tramline. The coils came in half-mile bundles, so we had at least fourteen eighty-pound coils to haul up the trail. Harold Holm was on that crew, a very capable, intelligent young man. One day he slipped on the glacier, slid quite a ways, hit a rock and injured his back. He didn't think it was bad, but it got worse and worse. After resting in camp, he worked for a couple of days, but the pain just got worse. Harold eventually had his back fused and ended up an invalid. Nowadays they could have fixed it. I always felt quite bad about that. We didn't have any crampons or ice axes. The way I saw it, Harold would have been all right if he hadn't hit that rock. He just would have slid a long way to the bottom of the basin."

At the end of September, with the top of the mountain blasted off and the materials for the cabin on top, the crew called it quits for the year. The next summer, Frank Benesch, who built practically every lookout cabin in the Snoqualmie National Forest, began work on the Three Fingers cabin. Benesch was experienced, but thought Three Fingers was something else. The standard cabin at that time was usually a twelve-foot square box with a cupola. The Three Fingers Lookout design was new, descriptively called the Grange Hall style. It had no cupola. Most importantly, it was fourteen-foot square, a fact that came as a surprise to Engles.

"The rock platform was barely twelve feet wide so the cabin was going to hang over the edge a bit. Headquarters didn't tell us about the size change and it made a big difference. It raised the dickens with us. The north and south sides had to be built up with flat rocks. The cabin was almost all pre-fab so that made Frank's job a bit easier. He could construct an entire side on the ground and stand it up without having to dangle out over the edge. There was one problem we didn't forsee. The lookouts would always have trouble opening the shutters on the north and south sides. I wasn't smart enough to deviate from the plan. I should have had the shutters open from the insides. Frank was just following instructions and we paid for it later."

In September of 1932 the cabin was finally ready for occupancy. It had been three years since Engles and Bedal had stood on the rock pedestal in the snow wondering whether or not to jump. It had been three years of hard, sometimes torturously back-breaking, work, but next summer the Darrington District would have an eye gazing over thousands of acres of heretofore unprotected forest. Looking back on past experiences, Albert Towne felt that few were more exhilarating or memorable than the summer he spent working on the Three Fingers lookout.

Harry Bedal, who had spent the better part of two summers on the mountain overseeing the operation, had good reason to be proud of the results. Harold Engles said, "Three Fingers was Harry's greatest achievement. But you ask me if he talked about it. It should be, 'Did Harry Bedal ever talk?' No, he didn't say much. Harry wasn't too imaginative. Some of us dream, Harry was strong. He just went out and did the job. What a nice way to be; just go out there and tackle things. I never thought much about what we'd accomplished. It was our work. I never for one moment doubted we'd have a lookout on top of Three Fingers after I decided to have it built. Now, the Seattle office had some questions, but I couldn't understand what all the fuss was about. When I was transferred down to Oregon, I never mentioned the cabin we'd stuck on top of that little piece of rock. I remember reading Catherine Eastwood's article in the *Saturday Evening Post* about Three Fingers and that gave me pause, but not for long. Lately though, I have given it some thought, analyzed the project.

"It was pretty amazing wasn't it?"

CHAPTER FIVE
The Lookouts — Harold Weiss, 1935

Fresh from visits with Harland Eastwood and Harold Engles, men who tower over me, I am not prepared to look down on Harold Weiss when he opens the door to his home. A garrulous man, with a hearty voice, he gives me a lively tour of the house. There is the cedar door, hauled out from the forests near the Whitechuck River, the trees, taken as saplings from various spots in the Cascades and the lookout cupola which sits atop the house. It gives him a view of his favorite mountains, Three Fingers, Pilchuck and, on occasion, Pugh. He tells me of the time he arranged with his brother to send signals by mirror from his lookout cabin on Pugh to a street on Everett. It worked.

There is a feistiness about Harold Weiss. He decided, while bedridden one spring, that he was going to become a mountaineer and he did. He decided he wanted to work for the Forest Service and he kept after the rangers until they gave him a job. "I was a small guy and had to work hard to keep up with those big guys, Bedal, Skaar, Engles and Eastwood."

Harold wears his love of the Cascades like a boutonniere in his lapel. He is not afraid to wax almost poetic about the mountains he first started exploring in his early twenties, almost sixty years ago: the views, the huckleberry bushes turning colors in the fall, the wildlife, the solitude. "I don't know of any mountain that doesn't have a great view", he exclaims. Weiss has a soft streak for the mountains. At times it seems as if he is speaking of a lost love. A hip injury has limited his hiking, but he sees a great deal of the outdoors from behind the wheel of his camper. "I always hit the high spots. That old camper went up on the highest mountain road in the world, Mt. Evans in Colorado. Kind of a rough road the last couple of miles, but it wasn't bad. The camper never coughed once. From Mt. Evans I looked down on Denver. That's all I've seen of Denver. I've never cared for big cities. I just stayed up in the mountains from northern Colorado to the southern part; some beautiful country, but I still think the North Cascades are more beautiful. Those saplings I brought from the mountains have grown so tall I can hardly see my mountains from the lookout. I think I'm just going to have to clip them."

****

Darrington is cold, wet and quiet in the winter. The town's economy, which ebbs and flows with the passing of the seasons, hibernates from late fall to early spring. Logging, Darrington's life breath, is limited to the snow-free lowlands, but for the loggers, bundled up against the cold, mucking around the damp forests, the work is hard and rarely productive. The town's other large employer, the National Forest Service, maintains a skeleton crew which oversees the logging, repairs equipment and performs other small administrative duties. The townsfolk, long used to the winter lull, have put away enough money, cut lots of firewood and canned a pantry's worth of food to see them through the lean months. Spring brings life to the Sauk, Suiattle and Whitechuck River valleys. Snow melt fills the streams and rivers. Pungent smells of wet cedar and lowland wild flowers mingle. Fields of tall grass glisten green in the warmer sun. Summer is in the air.

At the Darrington ranger station seasonal help is contracted to build and maintain mountain trails, clear brush along logging roads, fight fires and man fire lookouts. The lookouts will be the last to assume their duties. Fires are rare in June. Rain isn't. Snow still covers the trails leading to the cabins of Mt. Higgins, Pugh and the new lookout on Three Fingers. The tiny 14x14 wooden box with windows on its south peak appears occasionally in the swirling mists, wind blown snow packed against cabin walls, ice glazing the rocks and guy wires which struggle to keep the cabin earthbound in high winds. Winter eases its grip on the high mountains grudgingly. Three Fingers is the most remote of the Darrington District lookouts and the last manned every year. In 1935, its first year of operation, Harold Weiss did not walk through the lookout doorway until August 1st.

Lookout duty was a prized assignment and Mt. Pugh and Three Fingers were the plums. Harry Tucker, the last lookout on Three Fingers, said, "I always thought that Three Fingers was the ultimate. I felt, and I think the others did too, that we were the elite."

Few men possessed those qualities which marked them for a summer camped atop rugged peaks, isolated from the rhythms of daily life in the Stillaguamish Valley. During his term as district ranger, Harold Engles was always keeping an eye open for men able to handle lookout duty. It was frustrating packing a ranger and his summer provisions to the cabin only to find, after a few days, that the person was not suited for the job. Early one season Engles and a young lookout hiked up to Mt. Higgins to fix up the cabin for the summer. They spent twenty-four hours listening to several real-life melodramas unfolding in lookouts to the north.

"We were listening to the Baker River District. On Higgins you got real good reception. Every hour on the hour the Sourdough Mountain lookout repeated 'Sourdough to Desolation'. Those same three words five times, all day. Desolation Mountain was the point he was supposed to reach in order to make contact with the district office. The poor guy never got a hold of them, but he must have gotten in the habit because he kept repeating those same three words, 'Sourdough to Desolation'. If someone had answered he'd probably have fainted. That was funny, but it was only the beginning.

"The Baker River District had hired a young girl to man one of the lookouts. I'd seen her at the guard station. She was very attractive. I think her name was Rosemary. I figured the boys were going to be interested in her. The rangers were coaching her on the radio. They told her they'd drop supplies. They were very encouraging, telling her everything was going to be swell. Well, that night, we had one heck of an electric storm. I'm sure she hid under the bed. They all did; the only place a person couldn't see anything. On inspections I always checked under the bed; no dust. Each lookout was supposed to keep a record of all the lightning strikes, but I knew darn well they weren't. I'd ask, 'Who's been under here?'

"The next morning we heard Rosemary on the radio. All she said was, 'I'm coming down. I'm coming down.' The rangers gave her a long pep talk and when they'd finished, she said simply, 'I'm coming down.'

"Two hours later another voice from still another lookout came on the radio. 'There's a bear on the catwalk. What am I gonna do?' I turned to the lookout and said, 'Heck, instead of us paying you, you should pay us for this entertainment; this job's worth money.'

"The voice returned. 'What am I gonna do?' The bear was looking in the window at him, probably taking inventory of the cans and one fat lookout. The bear had walked up 30-40 feet of stairs to get to the catwalk. The rangers told him to poke it with a broom. He shot back, 'I'm not poking any bear!'

"Eventually the bear left . . . and so did the lookout. The Baker River district didn't have many more than a couple of lookouts and two of them left in one day. When it's someone else's grief, it's a tremendous joke. Had it been our district, I wouldn't have felt so hot."

Engles, who liked to work with his men in the forests, was usually able to determine which of his employees would make good lookouts.

"The lookouts had to see well. We gave them eye tests and they had to take a course. Butch Osborne wrote the booklets for the course, a tremendous character. Butch put together the booklets on observation and smoke chasing and they were real helpful."

There were many attributes for which no amount of training could compensate. Engles looked for men who had a familiarity with alpine conditions, had good mountain sense and could live in isolation for up to three months at a time. Engles was rarely disappointed with his choices for lookout duty.

He remembers one lookout he hired while working in Oregon, who had to be replaced after letting two fires "blow up" in his face. "Down in the valley we could see the smoke, but the lookout claimed there wasn't any fire. It was an unfortunate situation."

Engles jokingly added, "I should have known we'd have trouble when I saw his pink sleeping bag liner. Pink's not a man's color. It knocked out Jack Dempsey. I read an article about his marriage to Estelle Taylor, the actress. She finished the bedroom in pink and after that he wasn't worth a damn in the ring."

Harry Tucker liked to kid Harold about his theories concerning pink. "I always gave him a bad time. So did Anna May. She sometimes threatened to paint the bedroom pink while he was away on a hike."

Good lookouts were sometimes hard to find. Engles met Harland Eastwood, the second Three Fingers lookout, while on one of his marathon day hikes through the district. Harold Weiss got his job through persistance and Harry Tucker through word of mouth.

"Charles Thurston, the district ranger in the late 'Thirties and early 'Forties, came down to Tuckerville (near the base of Whitehorse). He was in search of a lookout and heard I knew Three Fingers pretty well. I was out back with my brothers making sling shots. I was barefoot and just wearing bib-overalls. I don't know how impressed he was but I got the job."

Dale Cole, the associate dean of the College of Forest Soils at the University of Washington, found employment in Darrington as the result of hitch-hiking. "I first climbed Three Fingers on my way from Verlot to Darrington in 1951. I was the lookout on Pilchuck with two days off and decided to hike across. I started hiking from Verlot (there were no roads at the time to provide easy access). I climbed to Goat Flats from Canyon Creek. I still remember arriving at Goat Flats at the same moment a rain storm arrived. I headed for a grove of trees to find some shelter. At that time of my life I didn't carry a tent or tarp. As if created for me, located within the grove of trees was the Goat Flats shelter. I had no idea the shelter existed.

"The next morning was beautiful, so I climbed up to the lookout. While on the summit, I saw a fire in the Jim Creek drainage. Believing that no one else had reported the fire, I picked up my pack and ran down to Boulder River, out French Creek to the highway. The first car that stopped to pick me up was a Forest Service rig. The driver was Harold Engles. Of course he knew about the fire. It was my hike from Verlot that caught his interest. On the spot he offered me a job for the next summer. As we headed to Darrington, he told me about some of the early hikes he had taken through the very same country. "The next spring I did find my way back to Darrington and asked Harold if he really had a summer job. He not only remembered our meeting the summer before, he obviously expected me to be working for him. That summer had to be the best a young man could ever have. It was the beginning of my serious interest in mountaineering and convinced me to go into forestry as my profession."

Harvey Manning, noted northwest author and outdoorsman, said "A lot of guys in my crowd lusted to get summer jobs with the Forest Service. Very few did. We, in Seattle, suspected you had to have pull. It seemed to me that a kid who came from a logging town and a logging, or Forest Service, family, got to the UW and took forestry, had a lock on the job."

Harold Engles acknowledged the college connection. "We were obliged to find work for two forestry students each summer and we did hire local fellows. But I looked for capable young men wherever I could find them."

There was probably no such thing as the typical lookout. He certainly wasn't Mark Trail. He, and on occasion, she, came in a variety of shapes and sizes, was sometimes gregarious, sometimes misanthropic. He was college educated and he was a local boy who matriculated at the university of the forest. He was strong and loved nature. He was small, but pugnacious and sometimes hid under the bed during an electrical storm. Perhaps the only common bond was the shared knowledge that lookout duty was special.

During the early weeks of summer, the lookouts worked in the lowlands, in Tucker's words, as "coolies, maintaining trails, fixing telephone lines," waiting for the lookouts to open. Engles liked to take new lookouts up and spend a day with them. "It was kind of a worry for anybody who was conscientious and we had imbued them with the importance of their job." One year, while helping the Higgins lookout pack up gear, he almost had to pack up the young man.

"The man's name was Franklin Fowler, a real nice fellow. He was new, and early on the trail he wasn't doing well at all. I took his pack and still left him in the dust. I reached the cabin about midday and by early evening had things ship-shape but still no Fowler. At dusk he came into view, almost crawling the last few yards to the cabin. Heck, I was the one with the pack. He crawled right into bed, but he stuck it out that summer. I remember telling him the next day that, during a spell of bad weather, he could come down for a day or two. He replied rather seriously, 'Listen, if I go down, I stay down.'"

The Three Fingers lookout was by far the most difficult to reach. It had taken over a full summer to construct in 1932 but had remained vacant until 1935. There weren't funds available to man it. The Depression reached even to the tops of the highest Cascade peaks.

Harold Weiss, the first lookout, had grown up in the Everett area but knew very little about the Cascade Mountains. In 1930, at age 23, Weiss made his first trip in the Cascade high country. "I was ill that spring and had a lot of free time. While lying in bed, I studied Forest Service maps and planned trips even though I'd never been in the mountains before. That summer I headed up to White Pass, southwest of Glacier Peak. The pack on my back was enough to kill a horse.

"I stayed in that area and met a sheep herder with thousands of sheep. I also hooked up with a party of young fellows who were going to climb Glacier Peak. I'd never done any mountaineering and didn't want to go alone. These kids were no more experienced than I and I ended up leading the party. I had all sorts of adventures that summer. I sprained my ankle over by Benchmark Mountain and had to use a stick for a crutch. The lookout let me stay for a few days while the swelling went down. The lookout life appeared pretty interesting. Most of that summer was spent in the mountains and I got hooked.

"Until 1930 I had been working at a lot of jobs, in the new pulp mill in Everett, fish canneries, but in 'Thirty-one I was geared up for a job in the mountains. I was so attached to the mountains by then. I kept after the people at Darrington, but every position was taken. One of the lookouts on Pugh had died and his replacement refused to go up, figuring he'd see the ghost of that old lookout. I jumped at the opportunity. I didn't even have a chance to go to the early spring school. Harold Engles called me up and told me to go so I went; just jumped right up on Pugh.

"Those were rough times in 'Thirty-one, you know. You talk about wages today, making $100 a day. I made $85 a month and had to buy my own food. I didn't get much work after the fire season. But each year there was a little more. I'd start earlier in the spring and get about six months. Of course wages improved a little but not a lot."

In the late spring of 1935 Harold Engles approached Weiss about manning the new Three fingers lookout. "I've got a new lookout," I told him. "It's a little more adventuresome, a little different. What do you think?"

Weiss accepted and found the hardest part of the job was clearing the trail to the cabin. "I helped Harland Eastwood get acquainted with the Pugh lookout and then I came back to Darrington and we began packing supplies to Three Fingers but we only got to Saddle Lake because of windfalls. I spent about two weeks clearing the trail and fixing the phone lines."

Once in the lookout, Harold's days were spent waiting, waiting for fires. That summer Weiss had no fires to report. It left him with a little free time and one day he decided to scramble up the north peak. "I got in between the middle Finger and the north and ran right up the chimney. There was no use taking a rope along. It didn't do me any good and I never uncoiled it. I was alone with no ice axe, no pitons, or anything. The glacier on Three Fingers was more open than it is today and you had to watch yourself. One day I was coming down to Tin Can Gap. It was easier to drop down on the glacier rather than follow the trail. I was heading down to pick up some supplies. I retraced my route the next day and found my tracks disappearing into a wide, deep crevasse. I couldn't see the bottom. How I got across without falling through, I don't know.

"Most of what I was packing in was food. I bought my food in Darrington and the packers would carry it up as far as possible using horses or mules. Then I had to backpack it up. I ate lots of beans and rice, but I had a fairly good menu for a man who didn't know anything about cooking. There were some canned goods, but during the Depression, you couldn't afford a lot of canned food."

Another of Weiss's duties was maintaining the telephone lines, his only link with the outside world. "I had to work the telephone lines from Goat Flats to the cabin, repairing and stringing out emergency wires. Sometimes I'd run into a herd of goats below Tin Can Gap. I remember once heading down the trail to the Flats. There was a big herd of them. They saw me and started moving down around a cliff. Two young kids started up the cliff and got stuck. A big Billy came up behind them and butted the two kids so hard I could hear them from where I stood; hit them so they'd turn around and go below the cliff. Those goats were a lot of fun; they weren't too scared.

"I don't recall ever seeing any bear on Three Fingers, but I've seen plenty of them in the forest. Once when we were working up the Goat Lake trail, we came across a big brown bear on the trail. We were all loaded down with saws and tools. He wasn't more than ten feet from us and we just stood there looking at him. He looked at us, he or she, whatever it was. Finally we decided to just ease on by and he didn't attack. We just got the hell out of there. You didn't want to yell and try to scare it that close. I remember once going up the old railroad track put in by the Sauk Line Timber Company. I was walking a trestle near Bedal and, below me walking the logs in the creek, was a big brown bear. I pussy-footed right above him and let out a big yell and I thought he was going to tear those logs all apart getting out of there."

Weiss's summer on Three Fingers was uneventful. There were no major fires or lightning storms and few visitors. There were occasions when the wind would kick up and lift the lookout "right off the ground." Weiss later spent several summers on Mount Pugh. "I guess I chose to go back to Pugh because it was my old homestead. I just loved Pugh. You got great views on Three Fingers but Pugh had the best."

After six years with the Forest Service, Weiss left. "I was seasonal, before there was any civil service. It's better now, but there was no future unless you had a forestry education. I'm convinced that the Forest Service should put more lookouts on these mountains and put the kids to work. It's not that expensive, not as expensive as building missiles and all these armaments and planes.

"I started building a house in 1935. It took a few years to build the darn thing. I built a cupola so I'd have my own lookout. The front door is made from a piece of cedar Nels Skaar and I cut up on the Whitechuck trail. It must have weighed almost two-hundred and fifty pounds and Nels and I carried it out. I'm not too big, but I liked to keep up with those big guys. Nels was a real woodsman. He could cut a two-foot windfall with an axe and it looked like it was done with a saw. That's one solid door. The rocks in the fireplace were collected in the Cascades and many of the firs on my property were carried out from Circle Peak, Cascade Pass and Hidden Lakes Peak.

"After I got married, I didn't get out in the mountains as often as I would have liked. I took my kids up on Pilchuck when they were just little snots. My son is a real mountain addict, but he can't get away very often. The last time I was up around Mt. Baker, before my wife was hurt in a car accident, we hiked up to Table Mountain. It's not much of a climb, but it was the first mountain she'd ever climbed. From up there it's a good view of Baker. I climbed Baker, but I never got up Rainier. It broke my heart to think about it; that I never got there while I was working for the Forest Service, while I was fit and able. Until I hurt my hip a few years ago, I would hike up Pilchuck if I couldn't get anywhere else. I must have been up there at least twenty-five times. It may not be big, but it's a mountain and, you know, they're all good. You never forget them entirely. You can become addicted to mountains. I never got addicted to whiskey but I am to these damn cigarettes. That was my mistake when I went up on Mt. Pugh the first time. I didn't know what I was going to do sitting up there all summer so I brought some Bull Durham along. I never smoked before I was 25. Then I started rolling cigarettes and that's how I accumulated the habit. Now it's a fifty-year addiction. No doubt it's harmful, but I'm still alive.

"I remember on Pugh, there was a steep east side, just like Three Fingers. There was a rock set up on top, about eight feet high. I wore tennis shoes to get around. I had some visitors up there and I was running around like a damn goat. I was standing right up on top. One woman closed her eyes. I was much more sure footed then. I wouldn't do it now. But, then, when do you ever get over being foolish? I haven't yet. Maybe in my next life I will have a little more sense."

Left to right, Robert Craig, Harland Eastwood and Harold Weiss on the summit of Indian Peak on Cascade crest near White Pass.

CHAPTER SIX

The Lookouts — Harland and Catherine Eastwood, 1936

As the ferry pulls into the slip at Lopez Island, I'm not sure what to expect. Harry Tucker, who has come along for the ride, last saw Harland Eastwood forty-seven years ago on Three Fingers. We've both heard from Harold Engles that Eastwood is not in good health, although on the phone he had sounded fine. Walking off the ferry, I look up to the small ticket office and see a big, white-haired gentleman. It is Harland.

He reaches out with his one arm and shakes my hand vigorously. He leads us to his truck and proceeds to give us a quick tour of the island. He easily shifts gears, maneuvering the truck along the winding country roads. He shows us historical plaques he made and voluntary carpentry work he has been doing. Harland's handiwork seems much in evidence around the island. He looks fine to me.

From the moment they meet, Harry and Harland are exchanging stories. Sandwiched between them in the truck, I yearn for a tiny tape recorder. Harland isn't afraid to express an opinion and doesn't care who knows how he feels. He often refers to his ornery streak. In some of the stories, it gets him into trouble. Other times it gets him what he wants. Harold Engles is acquainted with Harland's orneriness. "I gave Harland quite a talking to about some jobs that he hadn't gotten done. Harland just loved to roam more than work sometimes. But he'd just flash me this big grin. He still has that grin."

In the evening, Harland prepares us a hearty meal of chili with homemade blackberry pie for dessert. He shows the book he is working on, which will soon be published (it was published in the fall of 1983). He spent his early years at Fort Whitman, which sat on a small island in Puget Sound near Deception Pass. Years later he found there was almost no record of its existence. A government bureaucrat, at one point, refused to acknowledge that it had ever existed. It took long hours in libraries all over the country to dig up all the information he needed for the book. Harland is quietly proud of the book and Harry stays up most the night reading it.

Before we hit the sack, Harland shows us home movies he made on Three Fingers. They are almost fifty years old, but the quality is amazing. Much of the camera work was done by his wife, Catherine, who died about five years ago. He has not shown the films in some time and one senses that it is a bittersweet moment for him. He and Catherine shared so many adventures. There are scenes of Harland and Bob Craig skiing down from Tin Can Gap carrying 80-pound bales of telephone wire around their necks. He apologizes for his lack of style, fine parallel turns down the 40-degree slope, explaining, "Every time I turned, the bale shifted sides and threw me off-balance."

Like Harold Engles, Harland Eastwood still walks tall. Looking at the broad shoulders, it is easy to imagine him lugging 140-pound packs, swinging down ropes one-handed, or single-handedly building a bridge across Elliott Creek. As we are waiting for the ferry, Harland asks about Harold Engles. "You know, he looked fine the last time I saw him, but I've heard he isn't as sharp as he used to be." Harry glances at me, shakes his head and smiles.

****

Nature often laughs at the labors of Man. A gust of wind sends a floating bridge to the bottom of a canal, a rent in the earth's surface topples buildings, a volcanic eruption devastates miles of replanted timber. Every spring the trails in the Darrington district were blockaded by limbs and trees strewn like pick-up sticks across miles of forested pathways. For the Three Fingers lookout it meant weeks of arduous hacking and sawing before he would be able to open the cabin. For Harland Eastwood, the lookout in 1936, it was just one more challenge to accept. A hunting accident at age 17 left him with one arm. The doctor who amputated young Eastwood's right arm counselled him after the operation. "The doctor told me I had two choices. I could buy myself a cup, some pencils and let people take care of me or I could get on with my life, live it to the fullest."

Eastwood, who at seventeen stood well over six feet and weighed about two-hundred pounds, wasted little time on self pity. "That spring I turned out for track. I held the city high school record for the high hurdles in San Francisco until 1950. I played football at Galileo High School. One year I played quarterback. After football season I thought I would go and see the basketball coach. He said, 'Get out of here. I don't want no one-armed guy around here.' My dad was in the Army so I turned out for the basketball team at Fort McDowell. We traveled all over the state. One evening I scored seventeen points, quite a few for those days."

Harland rarely took no for an answer. He became an accomplished downhill skier and a member of mountain rescue at Mount Rainier. Eastwood never backed down from a challenge whether it was a steep mountain or a stick-shift truck.

After graduation from high school, Eastwood followed his parents to Seattle where he attended the University of Puget Sound; he also played football. During the summer he hiked and climbed in the Cascades, working a couple of summers in Mount Rainier National Park.

"The summer of 1932 I was climbing in the Monte Cristo area, Columbia Peak, when we ran into a group of young climbers bringing out a body. The kid had fallen on Monte Cristo Peak. We helped them carry the body out even though our group had little food and wanted to get home. They were all-in so we gave them a hand. Harold came by. He was on one of his long day hikes through the district. We chatted for a while on the railroad track and he asked me what I was doing in two or three days. I said, 'nothing' and he said, 'Do you want to work down in Verlot?' I told him yes, that I'd get right back.

"I worked at Verlot, built the first toilets at the campground, had help from the Shedeen brothers, two boys mining at Monte Cristo. They moved down to Silverton when working on the campgrounds. I remember we got $60 a month. We built some fire pits, a few tables and a couple of stoves. I drove a Model T Ford. There were actually no roads deep into the area. The Model T just kind of made its way through the woods. The next summer I ran around the campground, picking up garbage, that sort of stuff. One day I was working with James Galvin; he was the protective assistant at Silverton. He and I were jacking up a bridge, just above Verlot; they called it a shoefly. A bend plopped out of the bridge and hit him in the chin and he fell into the river. The river was high. You know how the Stillaguamish is in May, going like mad. I jumped in, grabbed him and got his head above water and we sailed down the river, bumping into rocks. We finally came to a little place in between some rocks and a sandbar. I drug the two of us in there and

I told Jimmy, 'I told you we were going to get hurt here.' He was one of those guys who dove right in and never thought where he was going or what was happening. Here was this great big bridge, took an awful beating in the winter and sure enough, it popped Jim on the chin and knocked him over."

Harland rarely minced words. He let people know where he stood, sometimes punctuating his opinion with a fist or flailing ice axe. "When that Noble boy was killed on Three Fingers in 1937, there were lots of reporters crowding in when we brought his body down. I just kept swinging my ice axe and they kept dodging me and we finally got him in the hearse."

By his own account, Harland is "ornery". On one occasion his ornery streak got him "canned". "One winter Catherine and I were working at Stampede Pass. The Forest Service called me up about March and said, 'We're sending a guy up. We want you to go someplace else. Leave your food there.'

"I said, 'No, I got about four-hundred dollars worth of grub here and I'm not going to do it.'

"He said, 'You're canned.' So when the tractor came up and took all the snow off the road, off we went to Lester and headed downtown."

More often Eastwood let his actions do the talking. During the famous search for Delmar Fadden, the young climber who in the mid-thirties fell to his death after making the first January solo ascent of Mount Rainier, Harland spent weeks on Mt. Rainier, in bitterly cold weather until the young climber's body was found high on the slopes of the Emmons Glacier. Often he took pleasure in surprising fellow workers with his exploits. "There are a couple of bridges on Elliott Creek that I put up over fifty years ago. They sent me up there alone because I was too ornery. I got me a big block and a piece of cable and a couple of turnbuckles so I put a wire up between two trees and brought my logs out. I had this block and tackle and I lifted it up a little bit. I got on the other side of the rope and I pulled these two stringers across and they never did know how I did that by myself. I put the stringers down and, with plenty of cedar around it, had a nice little bridge. I guess the bridge was still standing until a couple of years ago."

After another summer at Verlot, Harland moved to Darrington. In 1935 he manned the Mt. Pugh lookout and in 1936 he married Catherine Koch. They met while attending the University of Puget Sound. "It was raining quite a bit at school.

I'd seen Catherine around school, in classes, several times. I asked her if she wanted a ride to school. She said 'yes' and we started going together."

Catherine had grown up in Eastern Washington and, although a self-described tomboy, she was not familiar with the rigors of mountain travel. "We had been going together for two years," she wrote in a 1937 *Saturday Evening Post* article which detailed her honeymoon summer on Mt. Three Fingers. "Harland had spent the summer on Mt. Pugh. At the end of the season he came to see me at my home. 'I'm not going back alone next year', he stated. He put a lot of emphasis on the "alone". I assumed that was his proposal. Anyway, we were married the following May, just before fire season."

Catherine's sense of adventure almost matched Harland's (according to Harland, "She wanted to get away and she wanted a man who knew the mountains") and she enthusiastically responded when he told her his lookout assignment would be the remote Three Fingers cabin. "Harland told me we wouldn't see many people. It was a fourteen-mile climb to the cabin. But what did I care? After all, this was our honeymoon. I told Harland, 'You may have to pack me, too, but I'm going with you.'"

Harland drove her up to a spot near Arlington where they could see Three Fingers. When he pointed it out to her, she said, "Fine". Before leaving for Darrington, the couple climbed Pyramid Peak near Mount Rainier as a warmup.

"The idea of Three Fingers didn't bother us a bit," said Harland. "The main thing was, we were married. The Depression was too far gone and I was glad to get a job and that $100 a month looked pretty good."

Typical wet, June weather kept the newlyweds at French Creek, near the trailhead, for almost a month. "We stayed at what had once been one of the former ranger stations. We had a stable with four horses. After about two weeks, Catherine, Bob Craig, the lookout on Mount Higgins, the packer, Cactus Robinson and myself headed up Boulder Creek, clearing trail as we went. It took several days."

The group hacked their way to Saddle Lake where they spent several more days. There was still quite a bit of snow in the high country around Goat Flats. The packer, with his four mules, Fanny, Mabel, Satan and Red, deposited the Eastwoods' summer gear at Goat Flats. Cactus was a bit angry, Catherine

Harland and Catherine Eastwood,
honeymooning at the lookout, 1936.

guessed, "because we had planned for Mt. Pugh, a much shorter hike, and had so much stuff."

According to Harland, "Mabel was quite a character. She wanted to go all the time, just hated going to pasture. You never had to tie her up or anything. She would head out and be gone two to three hours in the evening. She always knew where to find feed. When we were going over snow, we'd let her go first and she'd find the holes around the rocks. She was seventeen at the time and they used her for many more years. She died at thirty-four."

The summer gear had to be packed from the Flats to the Three Fingers lookout. "We had an awful pile of stuff at the Flats. I'd make one trip in the morning, one in the afternoon. Each load weighed about seventy pounds. Catherine would carry loads of about thirty-five to forty pounds."

The couple and "young" Craig spent a lot of time fixing the telephone wires. "The wire was good up until about Tupso Pass. At that point it hung quite low and was down in places. Bob and I had to insulate it. We carried the wire in eighty-pound bales. Bob and I skied down from Tin Can Gap with these bales over our shoulders, very awkward. Bob was a real help stringing the line. It was steep rock and he was such a good rock climber. He'd climb that steep stuff like it was nothing. We'd string the line in the rocks through an occasional steel stake and insulator dropped in the cracks and away we'd go. We had these special pliers, about two feet long hitched to our belts. Bob would also climb up the trees to string the high lines."

Although Bob Craig and Harland did most of the work on the phone lines, Catherine pitched in. "I helped replace line too. Once I climbed up on a stump of a gnarled mountain cedar and held the wire clear of the brush while Harland pulled it tight over a rock ridge and disappeared. I stood there for a long time, balancing with arms outstretched. It made me feel like a fancy radiator cap ornament."

"After a while I got pretty tired of it and called Harland. He didn't answer so I let out a whoop. In a few moments he came scrambling back down to look at me from the ridge.

"'When can I let go of this thing?' I pleaded.

"'Why fifteen minutes ago', he told me puzzled. 'I didn't know you were still there.'"

The Eastwoods lived in the Goat Flat shelter for a couple of weeks. Catherine marveled at the panorama and concluded

The Three Fingers glacier.

that one could "happily go blind watching the sunsets from the meadows." The lean-to leaked, even in the 1930's, but Harland devised a way to keep rain out as well as unwanted visitors. "We had a couple of pieces of an old tent that I stole down there at Darrington and we put those inside like a curtain for a little privacy. We were on our honeymoon!"

It was the middle of July before the Eastwoods finally moved into the lookout cabin. Catherine's first good view of the lookout came from the glacier. It appeared perched on the high rock like "some mysterious lamasery high in the Himalayas."

After the summer's gear was packed to the cabin and the lookout readied, the days passed slowly and peacefully. Harland remembers, "We'd wake up around four or five in the morning, take a good look around, then go back to bed for a little while. We'd have a leisurely breakfast and unless we had to visit the bathroom, we'd just stay around the cabin."

The Three Fingers outhouse is perhaps the most spectacular in the entire Cascade Range. Dropping hand-over-hand down a rope, one would come to a huge alcove on the sheer east face; a balcony seat to glorious views of Glacier Peak and Squire Creek, 2,000 feet below.

"We got our water at the lower edge of the last snow field about two-hundred yards below the cabin. I used to bring up two five-gallon cans, about seventy pounds. On a warm day Catherine would wash her clothes, lay them on the rock and they'd be dry in minutes.

"We stashed our eggs and cheese in cans in the snow. We used cans because some rodent would dig in the snow and eat food that wasn't locked up tight. We had some coneys and marmots for neighbors. They were pretty shy, not like the one on Mt. Pugh, which would sit by the door and squeal and squawl at you.

"There were cougars we could hear down in Copper Creek, some 2,500 feet below. When the wind was right, their mournful sound carried up to our cabin. A couple of old goats would follow Catherine wherever she went, all the way to Goat Flats. I think they'd been kicked out of the herd. It happens in herds like that. They were getting old and couldn't fight anymore. We'd watch them from a distance butting heads and, my gosh, the speed with which they hit! You could almost feel it in your bones."

The Eastwoods had 14 human visitors that summer. Friends

brought oranges and steaks, a real treat. One couple, the Varners who lived on French Creek, brought their nine-month-old baby. She was carried in a papoose. Mrs. Varner helped Catherine finish a sweater she was knitting. "I reached a point where it was ready to come off the needles when I realized that I didn't know how to stop. The project stagnated until a woman visitor showed me how to make a finishing row."

Harry Tucker remembers visiting the lookout when he was 15. He was accompanied by his brother, Jim, Dan Smith and Jack Watson and the Tucker dog, Cinder.

"We were on the glacier and having trouble getting our dog up one of the steeper snow slopes. Harland must have thought we were in trouble because he came down to help. Mrs. Eastwood was real cheerful. She gave us some jello. We weren't used to such delicacies and thought she was a great cook. When we got back to the trailhead, my dad was there to pick us up. He'd stopped at old Joe Gerkman's cabin and Joe always made you sample his homemade wine, pretty awful stuff. Dad rolled the car on the way out, but the only injury occurred when I stepped on Jack's shoulder getting out of the car. I broke his collarbone."

The Eastwoods stayed in contact with the lookouts on Mt. Pugh, Higgins and French Point. "One night three lookouts on three different mountains tried to sing harmony on a song over the radio. Some evenings we'd be entertained by harmonicas or ukuleles."

Catherine also recalled taking a great deal of kidding on the telephone, although "some of them would ring up quite seriously and ask for recipes. They'd ask for the chief cook."

One day Harland, using his 40-power telescope, focused in on the Mt. Higgins lookout manned by Bob Craig. He went to the phone and rang the unsuspecting lookout. "See here, young man", he exclaimed in mock indignation, "don't you know it's indecent to lie outdoors where people can see you like that?" According to Catherine, "It was a very startled young nudist, thinking himself miles from nowhere, who answered the phone."

Although visitors were few, Harland says, "We never got lonely. We were just happy as larks up there. Sometimes the mist would move in for a week and you couldn't see anything and we didn't like to go out on those rocks because they were slippery, so we'd stay in the cabin. When the weather was good we'd sometimes go on hikes. I climbed over to the north peak but didn't climb it. I didn't want to tackle that steep rock alone. Catherine never went anywhere I couldn't see her from the lookout, just in case she fell. Catherine and I had some short skis and with those things on, boy, you could get over to Tin Can Gap in a hurry.

"There were several storms that summer, some snow and ice and lots of wind. Sometimes when the kerosene stove wasn't working, which was about half the time, we'd just stay in our sleeping bags. It was mostly ingenuity that kept that stove going.

"We didn't see many fires. I would say the lookout was poor for spotting fires. It was too high and fog would cover the valleys. You could spot lightning fires on ridge tops. During electrical storms you could see the electricity dancing up and down the guy wires. The only other place I ever saw that was on St. Elmo's Pass on Mt. Rainier."

Catherine vividly recalled that storm. "Ominous clouds had moved in from the south. Harland looked at the clouds suspiciously but said nothing and we went to bed. I was used to the wind and rain and that didn't worry me, but in the middle of the night, I was dimly aware that the telephone kept ringing. After a while I realized Harland was up. He came over and said, "You'd better wake up. It's getting bad."

"I sat up sleepily, feeling very strange. There was something wrong. I raised my hand to my head. My hair was standing on end, literally. I pushed it down and it jumped right up. Wind and rain beat against the windows. Every time the lightning flashed the telephone rang. The room glowed with a strange light. I peered outside and saw that every guy wire looked like a neon sign. Electricity crackled up and down the cables. The very rocks shone with a weird illumination. St. Elmo's Fire."

The Eastwoods hastily moved all metal objects to one end of the cabin to prevent lightning from jumping about in case of a direct hit. The gasoline supply was moved from under the bed to outside the door. The radio was shut off to prevent destruction. Lurleen Simpson, a lookout on Mt. Pugh during World War II, was in the process of shutting off the radio when a direct hit blew the entire set off the airwaves.

It was a long night for the Eastwoods. Harland had to stay awake as long as the storm loomed overhead. Just before dawn the dark clouds moved on and the lookouts were able to get some sleep.

With the coming of early September frosts, the Eastwoods realized that they would have to close their honeymoon cottage. A dismal rain/snow storm made their last day somewhat less than poignant. "I was carrying a 130-pound pack and, from Tin Can Gap, Catherine carried a hundred pounds. She was in pretty good shape by the end of the summer. Despite the downpour, Catherine left with a certain amount of regret. They spent other summers in less lofty lookouts but she never returned to Three Fingers.

Harland and Catherine's life of adventure together, which included other summers spent on the French Point lookout, a stint on ski patrols and as partners in an outdoor manufacturing company, ended in 1980 when Catherine died. Harland, still ornery and active at 81, lives on Lopez Island in the San Juans. In 1983 he wrote a book on old Fort Whitman in Puget Sound and piloted a boat across the Gulf of Mexico in 1984. He does a lot of volunteer carpentry work.

Harland has found a new companion in adventure, Esther Carhart. His new wife and he bought a Volkswagen camper in 1984 and toured Europe. This past summer they served as volunteers for the National Park Service at Mount Rainier. They worked out of a cabin at White River Campground, the same one he manned fifty years ago. Eastwood loved the experience. In recounting the summer to a Seattle Times reporter, a bit of the Eastwood's orneriness crept in. Describing the tourists he and Esther met, he said, "You wouldn't believe this one guy, driving around the mountain for over an hour on a perfectly clear day, who said, 'Would you tell me where the mountain is?' and I said 'You might try looking out the window of the car.'"

Three Fingers lookout, 1941.   — Harry Tucker photo

CHAPTER SEVEN

The Lookouts: Robert Craig, 1937-1940

Robert W. Craig is sometimes confused with another Robert W. Craig, the noted alpinist and author of *Storm and Sorrow*. When I first started work on this book, I was confused. So was Harry Tucker. One afternoon we speculated on the possibility of Craig, the Three Fingers lookout being "that" Robert W. Craig. Harry got on the case and a couple of weeks later he wrote me a letter that poured cold water on our theory. Checking another expedition book, *K-2: the Savage Mountain*, Harry found that "the" Robert W. Craig had been 28 in 1953. "That would have made him thirteen years old when he first manned the Three Fingers lookout. Seems implausible, but the coincidence is remarkable: both Craigs, mountaineers, same first names, last names and middle initial. I Love a Mystery."

Hearing this, I was disappointed, having thought that "the" Robert W. Craig would have added a lustre of importance to the book. I confessed my disappointment to Harold Engles who said, "He may not have been the famous Craig, but in his own way, Bob Craig was as competent a mountaineer as the other guy, just a little more quiet about it all." Harold was right.

I have not met Bob Craig. We have corresponded through the mail and over the phone. I have seen him on film at Harland Eastwood's home. The fifty-year old celluloid reveals a young man, wiry, strong, agile and quietly confident. He skiied flawlessly down the steep slopes of Tin Can Gap, quickly front-pointed with crampons up a tall fir tree to hook up telephone wires and effortlessly pulled himself up a steep rock face below the summit.

After his four years on Three Fingers, Craig applied those same skills to mountain climbing, engineering and the running of his two-acre vineyard. But Bob Craig is a private man. Self promotion is anathema to him. He seems to take solitary pleasure in his accomplishments, relishing the doing rather than the telling. He has great admiration for those who do, including many of his associates in the Forest Service, who as he says "lived close enough to real pioneer times, that they still did what they could with what they had at hand: hard physical labor, diversity, the ability to cope, alone if necessary, with everyday, everyman stuff. No medals. The circumstances, the things to work with, all change. People do not change, but their basic training does. Take away chain saws, helicopters, short wave radio and try to man a Copper Mountain, Sourdough, Desolation or even Three Fingers today. I sound five steps to the right of Goldwater. Perhaps I'd better stop."

I think Bob Craig would want me to relate his story with as much precision and accuracy as possible. To tell of the doing without adding frills, without making a fuss over the man.

****

The Three Fingers lookout, isolated as it was, occupying such a dizzying perch and vulnerable to the often violent vagaries of Nature, required a guardian with the soul of an explorer; one who could put up with the long hours of enforced solitude, welcome the unexpected and defy heights. Robert Craig, who served as the Three Fingers lookout for four summers, 1937-40, inherited such an adventurous spirit from his father, Fred, who in the late 1890's traveled to the Yukon in search of gold.

Fred Craig and other teenaged friends pooled their money and bought a small herd of cattle which they shipped to Haines, Alaska, prodded over the infamous Chilkoot Pass and ferried down the Yukon River to Whitehorse. They arrived with lots of cattle and no money but were able to trade the cattle for claims. It was the beginning of a mining career that would see as many fat times as lean. Craig met his wife in the Yukon and in 1910 they moved to Fairbanks shortly after hearing news of a big strike there. Robert was born in Fairbanks in 1915.

"My dad had a poor opinion of Alaskan schools, so he sent my brother and me to school in Seattle." Bob attended the University of Washington where he initially majored in forestry. "I cruised timber in the Blue Mountains in the summer of 1934 and, in 1935, I applied for work in Darrington. The Darrington rangers didn't have a very high opinion of college boys, but the word from Bellingham was to take on one University of Washington student."

Harold Engles remembers with a chuckle being reluctant to hire the young college student, but soon found him to be a most capable employee and hardy outdoorsman. "I wasn't too enthused when he first arrived, just another one of those college punks we had to educate. But Bob was young, interested and just getting warmed up." After a summer on Mt. Higgins Craig moved to Three Fingers. "I was chosen in 'Thirty-seven as no one else would have it. The last three years I asked for the duty.

"Cactus Robinson was the packer all the years I was on Three Fingers. He called it 'Little America'. Cactus was a good packer, but he hated Three Fingers with a passion. I brought in supplies to last three months, an expenditure of about fifty to sixty dollars and hoped I would come out about right. I had a half-case of eggs that got a little strong by late August. It bothered the visitors, not me. Cactus would get the supplies as far as he could, Goat Flats, Tin Can Ridge or, if snow permitted, Tin Can Gap. I would drop down in the evening or during rainy weather about once a week to replenish the larder."

Once settled in, Craig began the waiting and watching. "Three Fingers was not a good lookout in those days. There was no logging in sight, no settled areas, not too much foot travel. I tried to give the area a good scan several times an hour, but it tended to be self cancelling because a lightning storm that was localized enough to produce fires that were truly your babies would also chop the phone line into little chunks. By 1940 I had a good shortwave radio which helped immensely.

"There were usually one or two storms each summer. If I was lucky, they bypassed the peak. One storm, I think in 1939, hit the peak square on and from 8 p.m. until 2 a.m. the next morning, I tallied about six-hundred strikes within fifteen miles, several hitting the house. Rain usually damped out most fires although there were two, one at Goat Flats and one on Meadow Mountain, that I had to run down and put out.

"St. Elmo's Fire, the static discharge of the ground-to-cloud (or vice versa) is spectacular in the night. Each point of rock about the house had its own little blue flame, rising as the charge built up, winking out when lightning struck. One became apprehensively expert at judging when the next strike was coming by gauging the length of the flame. What you could not know was where the next strike would hit. A strike five miles away would extinguish all static flames, so also would a strike on the lightning rod six feet over your head. The latter was more impressive. St. Elmo's fire occurred during the daylight but not visibly so. It was there and, wind permitting, you could hear it, a steady hissing. I once saw a kestrel make repeated attempts to land on a point of rock during such a discharge. He never did set down successfully. After that wild storm there were so many fires in the flats below me, it looked like a gypsy camp.

"I was rather conscientious about occupying the station except when weathered in. Occasionally I would run about, explore a bit. I found a rock formation several hundred feet due south of the cabin, a man's profile. I called him the Aztec. He faced due east overlooking Clear Creek. I hope he is still there. If he broke off, he didn't stop for one-half vertical mile, so near to vertical as to make no nevermind. I have seen the Aztec wearing fifteen-inch plumes of St. Elmo's Fire when the mountain was hot.

"A very interesting trip was to circumnavigate the mountain clockwise at the base, crossing beneath the glacier, under and west of the north peak, around the three small lakes (now known as Craig Lakes), to the Squire Creek watershed, along the shelf meadows at the base of the east wall, through a notch, perhaps a mile south southeast of the lookout and back up.

"There used to be a bear den at the foot of the north peak which was repeatedly used for hibernation. It was also quite possible to go directly from the lookout to the north peak; only the first two-hundred feet were hairy.

"I had an excellent single-hole john built along the route to the north peak. As it involved stemming down a rock crack for some ten or twelve feet (I had a rope for the city types), it did not get all the use it should have from visitors. After I left it may have never again been used. Solidly built of scrap two by fours and a hand-carved apple box end, it survived the four years I spent there. Drafty perhaps, but with five-hundred foot pit, you did not have to move it yearly. Visitors never appreciated it."

More often than not Craig's visitors were of the four-legged and winged variety.

"There was a resident colony of packrats on the peak as, oddly, there are on many high peaks. We maintained a very amicable relationship. They were not let into the house except during lightning storms. Outside the static electricity would puff them up to a startling size. It must have been uncomfortable as they seemed to welcome my leaving the door ajar and soon there would be a small, well-behaved, crowd in there.

"Migrants, probably the young expanding out of a crowded territory, often crossed the ridge from the Squire Creek side westward. One of my best looks at a Saw Whet Owl came there and once I found a red squirrel perched on the ridge top wondering where to go from there. He was a good mile from the closest trees. Ptarmigan were everywhere and quite tame. I had some very unsuccessful planter boxes outside the door which they used for dust baths. They, and also the Grey Crowned Finches, did not come onto the glacier or snow fields until dusk, I believe, because of eagles and hawks. The storm winds and general updrafts carried many insects and seeds and left them on the colder surfaces, food for the birds. Between Tin Can Gap and Tin Can Ridge along the trail, neither goats nor ptarmigan were alarmed in foggy weather by my travel. The goats would get off the trail fifty to a hundred feet and so long as I didn't stop, just slowed down, they would just watch me. Ptarmigan would not move more than ten feet off-trail.

"My best look at a Golden Eagle was on Three Fingers. At every station he occupied longer than a week, Harold Weiss built a canvas and board reclining chair. I was slumped in this one reading *War and Peace* (at that age I thought it was necessary and the lookout provided the quiet and leisure), feet up on the bunk, facing east. I became aware of some slight movement and fortunately only moved my eyes. Outside the window not more than ten feet away, riding the perpetual up-draft of the east face, was a Golden Eagle. The size of the windows are ten by fourteen inches and it speaks volumes for his aerodynamic control when I say he stayed, soaring, within one pane for several minutes, not leaving until I reached for my camera.

"I used several *Saturday Evening Posts*, probably left by Catherine Eastwood, making paper airplanes. One out of ten would be properly designed to keep turning in a circle and remain stable until no longer visible. The eagle, which had a nest somewhere on the north peak, would follow them up, at a larger circle, baffled, I presume, by this strange bird that showed no fear. They never attacked. I probably littered much of Squire Creek Basin until I ran out of Saturday Evening Posts.

"One summer I brought my dog, Perry, all sixty-five pounds of him up to the lookout. He was a good dog and would go all day with a ten-pound pack on his back, but he was not a good Three Fingers dog. His basic house training was too thorough; he would not relieve himself outside the door. Both front and rear yards of the lookout he included within house limits. I had to carry him down and back up the ladder three to four times per day. Below Goat Flat he had a great knack for locating bear cubs which he would chase up a tree. As he ranged several hundred feet in front of me, this invariably wound up with an anxious sow bear charging out of the brush. At me, not Perry. I was generally off on some trail maintenance job with axe, packboard, cross-cut saw, et cetera. I would run like a deer, with the packsack beating my brains out. My father always said, 'Stand your ground. She's only bluffing.' I am not the man my father was. I ran. All you had to do was indicate that you would run and the sow would stop. Five times in one August that happened. Perry thought it was a big joke.

"We usually closed the cabin in September, a miserable job, invariably in a driving rain. The north and south faces of the house were not accessible. That made taking down shutters an adventure. With wind and rain in your face, there was no clothing scheme that prevented either you or your pack from being soaked by the time you reached Goat Flats or much earlier. But comfort is a relative thing. By the time you reached the big timber below Saddle Lake, out of the wind, the only rain dropping second hand from the trees, your clothes soaked warm to body temperature and your mental condition a numb state, you were almost comfortable."

After four summers on the mountain, Craig left the field of forestry for engineering although he continued to explore the mountains. He climbed the Washington volcanos, skiied down Mt. St. Helens and in the 1940's attempted Mt. McKinley, reaching 17,000 feet before being blown off by storms. Today he and his wife, Elizabeth, own a small vineyard which occupies most of their days and, on occasion, their nights. Forty-five years after his last summer on Three Fingers Craig says: "The scenes still come back so vividly, rock by rock, that I am a little startled when I count back and find that it is a half-century since I first saw the mountain. Things were more vivid at that age. It was something that should have been done twice, not four times, but those last two summers, I quit better paying jobs just to go back to Three Fingers."

CHAPTER EIGHT

The Lookouts: Harry Tucker, 1941-1942

Until his bicycle accident eight years ago, Harry Tucker made an annual pilgrimage to his former summer home. Three Fingers is a special place for Harry, a storehouse for the dreams of youth and it is apparent that he dearly misses those trips to the lookout. But if there is melancholy in his voice when he talks of Three Fingers and the mountains, it is offset by his good humor. Speaking with a slight drawl he says he picked up from the Tarheels who live in Darrington, Harry will spin a yarn and when the listener exclaims with eyes wide, "Really?", he'll chuckle and say, "Nah, I was just kidding". Physical inactivity has put Harry several pounds over his prime hiking weight and gives him the look of a plump elf, a mischievous elf to be sure.

Harry is one of the great put-on artists. Luckily for him, his wife, Eileen, laughs at most of his jokes, although she often sighs in mock exasperation, "Oh, Harry." One time his penchant for kidding almost got him into trouble. Showing the visitor a snapshot of a body lying half under a steam roller, Harry's somber as he says, "This is kind of an unfortunate deal. A contractor parked a roller up the street and some kids were playing around in the evening and evidently one of them pulled the wrong lever and the thing rolled ahead and . . ."

Noting the terror in my eyes, Harry chuckles, "Nah, just kidding. My son and I got to looking at that roller. We took an old pair of pants and some shoes and stuffed them with pads and jammed it under the roller. For the finishing touches, I got a bottle of ketchup, sprinkled it around and then we went home and kind of forgot about it. Early the next morning my wife came in, whiter than a sheet and said, 'A lady says that roller parked up the street evidently ran over somebody last night.'

"I couldn't smile, laugh or anything. My wife had taken it seriously. I couldn't say a word because I was bound to get in trouble. So I said, 'Well, heck, let's go up and look at it.

My son and I walked up the street, looked real hard at the pants under the roller and then pulled them out. I muttered, loud enough for my wife to hear me, 'These damn neighbor kids.'"

Harry's enthusiasm for this book matches mine and he becomes archivist, editor, fact finder and cheer leader. I could not ask for a better partner. He accompanies me on a trip to Lopez Island to visit Harland Eastwood. By midnight the two of them are still exchanging stories. Harry ends up doing most of the interviewing. Letters from Harry are always witty and articulate, usually concluding with an invitation to 'come on up and visit sometime'. His enthusiasm is welcomed during those times I despair of ever finishing the book.

In August I move to Connecticut and after I have finished a couple of chapters, I give Harry a call to tell him the good news and let him know I'm ready to embark on the toughest chapter yet, his. Eileen seems strangely dispirited and hesitates before telling me that Harry had died a month earlier. I am as sad as I have ever been, but as I hang up, I envision Harry, loosed from a body that just couldn't keep up with his spirit, hovering nearby. I feel his presence as I struggle with his chapter. I hear his good-natured chuckle when I tell friends how Harry signed the cabin register when he opened the lookout in 1942. The register had a space marked "Destination" and under it Harry had scribbled, "God Only Knows!" I half expect him to jump in and drawl, "Nah, I was only kidding."

****

Darrington, situated a stone's throw from a number of rugged Cascade peaks was, in the 1920's, a long, bumpy ride from the cities on the Sound with their movie houses, department stores, amusement parks and sports arenas. What was there for an energetic youngster to do on a sunny Saturday? Well, there were the mountains, with their streams for fishing, forested hillsides for hunting and hiking and the snowy summits for climbing and skiing. In the 1920's, the trails, which led into the heart of the Cascades started virtually on the outskirts of Darrington. The woods were a fort, the peaks a castle; a natural playground for many children like Harry Tucker, Three Fingers' last lookout, who grew up in the shadow of Whitehorse, Higgins, Prairie and Jumbo.

"I was born at Clear Creek ranger station in 1920. My dad was working for the Forest Service at the time. Heck, I almost died there. My parents were going berry picking and almost decided to leave me napping at the cabin. I was just a baby. They figured it was best to take me along and, while we were gone, the cabin burned to the ground. It was a pretty spectacular fire, although Edith and Jean Bedal, riding their horses in from the Bedal place, raced right by without even noticing. They found out about it in town and Jean said, 'We were riding pretty fast.'

"Except for a brief stay in Woodinville when Dad tried to get into the goat rearing business, my family (six boys and a girl) were brought up in Darrington at Tuckerville. Dad homesteaded west of town right at the base of Whitehorse. Matter of fact, the south boundary of his spread was the National Forest line. We had a great life growing up. We never had much, but that big mountain was practically at the back door, so our hobby got to be climbing Whitehorse every spring. It became a yearly ritual.

"I remember a couple of years climbing it at least six times. I think I was a freshman in high school the first year I tried and it was pretty scary. We didn't have any climbing or camping gear. We'd use sticks to stop ourselves on the snow. Most of the time we'd do a standing glissade or just let go and slide down on the seat of our pants. One time my brother Dave made it to the top of Whitehorse in a little over four hours; that's a good 6,500 feet of elevation gain. I did it once in four-and-a-half hours but, heck, we weren't competing. We were usually just trying to catch up with the rest of the gang. Everyone except my mother climbed Whitehorse and Mom was a good hiker. I climbed that mountain at least one-hundred times. Makes me tired thinking about it. Our family didn't have super transportation, and it wasn't common to drive into Darrington. Whitehorse, being right behind us, became our entertainment. Once in a while I'd go north, wade across the Stillaguamish and climb Round Mountain or Higgins.

"It just seemed natural for us to be in the mountains, and everyone in the Tucker clan worked in the forests at one time or another. We all worked full or part-time for the Forest Service. Dave, Tom and Bayard pretty much made careers of it. Jim's a meteorologist for the Department of Natural Resources. My sister was a lookout on Mt. Pilchuck and now she and her husband are in the outdoor recreation business. My mom was a trail cook and later a lookout.

"I first started working for the Forest Service in my junior year of high school. I went out on a bunch of forest fires and was paid thirty-seven and a half cents per hour which for those days wasn't so bad. Of course there was lots of grub. I saved up enough money to buy a twenty-dollar Sterling down sleeping bag and it looked about the size of two loaves of bread. My dad used it once and couldn't believe something that small could keep him so warm.

"My brothers, some friends and I used to ski into places like Kennedy Hot Springs and Goat Flats in the winter. We had some modified skis and canvas socks and we used the skis like snowshoes. Talk about a clumsy deal.

"One Christmas vacation we spent three days at Goat Flats. It snowed and the wind never stopped blowing. We didn't have a stove, and the snow would whirl around and get inside our blankets. It was just miserable. We couldn't sleep at all and in the morning we'd get up and do some exploring just to keep the blood circulating. It's a wonder we all didn't die. We did get a little cranky and one of us got a little frostbite. I sure wish I'd had my down bag then.

"On our trips we always hoped for good weather because we never took a shelter, not even a tarp. Sometimes we'd camp in the alpine country, the clouds would move in and we'd lay in bed hoping it wouldn't rain. About midnight the first drops would hit us in the face and we'd wake up thinking kind of bleak thoughts, trying to figure out where the nearest trail was. The food was never too hot either.

"There were two teachers in Darrington, Mrs. Fleming and Mrs. Shipley and they took a bunch of us young guys on a week-long hike in the Glacier Peak area. We were all heavy eaters and damn near starved to death. Mrs. Fleming was a little overweight so she didn't mind because she was going to lose a little weight. One night we hit camp and the ladies broke out two cans of tomatoes and dumped in some salt, lots of water and then gave us five crackers each. That was dinner!

"My brothers and I also hiked around Glacier Peak and climbed it. We didn't use ropes or ice axes. I can't recall owning any mountain climbing gear until Jim and I got into college.

"The summer of my senior year at Darrington High School, I fought fires. There was a whole series of them that year and it seemed like the whole town turned out for them because fire fighters got fifty cents an hour, trail builders thirty-eight cents, which included room and board . . . lots of room. They'd give you a blanket and you slept under the trees. The food was pretty tasty, too.

"Next summer I worked in the Civilian Conservation Corps. I needed the money to get started at the University of Washington. I had just finished working for the CCC's, when Charlie Thurston, the district ranger, came around to Tuckerville and wanted to know if I would be interested in going up on Three Fingers. I said sure.

"By 1941 I'd been up Three Fingers several times; the first time in 1935. Harold Weiss was the lookout. We were all fifteen years or younger and we weren't used to an old geezer like Harold. He was almost thirty. We asked him the name of a little lake and he rattled off some names that turned the air blue. It was a pretty colorful description. He kind of intimidated us, just like the mountain did, but that night he came down to Goat Flats, shared some rice and beans and stayed the night. I met the Eastwoods and Bob Craig on climbs of the mountain and I looked forward to working on Three Fingers. Finding fires sure beat fighting them

"Each summer I'd get out of school, get up to Darrington and spend a couple of weeks sawing and cutting logs that had fallen across the trail. Such misery! I'd open the lookout about the middle of July and be on my way down by the middle of September. I'd have to hustle down to the UW and get a job before school started. There was an old-time grocer in town, a real pioneer who'd pack groceries and supplies for us. He'd pack the food so it could be put on the horses. I'd have to wait until I got my first check before I could pay him. I got about $150 a month. It was quite a deal figuring out supplies because you couldn't come running back to Darrington if you forgot something.

"We usually worked a week on the Boulder River trail. That was the bad part, sawing through those huge cedars which had blown down. We also had to repair the telephone lines knocked down by snow and falling tree limbs. The telephone was the old hand-crank type. Along the trail you'd call in every so often, using a regular little lineman's phone, to make sure everything behind you was clear. Once we were repairing line near Bear Cove (about one mile below Saddle Lake). The line at that point hung over a cliff above the trail, maybe fifteen to twenty feet. I climbed a tree next to the break and sunk my spurs into the trunk. My legs were also very sweaty, which meant I had a real

Harry Tucker descends hand-over-hand from the lookout to the col between the south and middle peaks.

Harry Tucker takes in the view of Goat Flats and beyond.

With the lookout closed in World War II, Harry's mother, Grace Tucker, with Harry's three younger brothers, spent the summer of 1943 in the Goat Flats cabin, serving as fire lookout and airplane spotter. Brothers Bag and Tom are pictured.

The lookout in 1955, shutters closed. — Harry Tucker photo

Three Fingers lookout, 1941, shutters raised. — Harry Tucker photo

good ground. I was hanging over this little cliff trying to splice the broken line. It was hard work and, just as I was pulling the wire together, some idiot in the district got on the deal and cranked the phone. That gave me a good jolt, but I didn't want to let go of all that work. I just hoped he'd get through on the first ring, but he didn't. My partner stood on the trail laughing himself silly. It wasn't dangerous, just painful and shocking. Everytime I hike past that bend in the trail, I remember that ringing phone.

"Most of our supplies were left at Goat Flats including five gallons of kerosene for the stove. One year the packer lugged up a lot more than we needed, but I packed it up to the lookout anyway. Heck, I was young, in good condition and always looking for something to do. It was a good excuse to get away from the cabin. The assistant district ranger was good about that. He'd call and say, 'Well, Harry, maybe you better get some of that kerosene'. I also left some of my grub at Goat Flats because it gave me a chance to roam around. One time it got me in trouble with a bear.

"One afternoon I hiked down to Goat Flats and as I reached the meadows, I noticed a trail of powdered cocoa. Then I found the box, milk cans and safety matches scattered all over. I hadn't left anything hanging up in the shelter. That bear must have just wandered in, smelled the milk (the pack horses always seemed to run into a bunch of yellowjackets, then take off through the trees and bang up the supplies, sometimes leaving me with leaky milk cans), chomped on a can with his canines and then was off to the races. He cleaned me out of canned milk. Doggone, I saw that bear later. He wasn't mean, just a scrawny little bear, but that didn't help me any.

"I had some friendly pack rat neighbors at the cabin. All the lookouts did. Those critters were company and lots of times I'd leave the door open and here'd come one of the pack rats. I'd leave them stew and sometimes, when one of them walked in, I'd close the door. We got along fine although I know some visitors to the lookout have complained about them. In the early 'Seventies somebody closed the lookout and deliberately locked in the pack rat. Next spring you could see where the poor old guy had tried to gnaw at the cabin corners trying to get out. We found him curled up in the center of a bunch of blankets. My daughter, Pat, got really mad about that and we left a note in the register asking people to be nice to the pack rats.

"One day in 'Forty-one, I crawled under the cabin (that's where the pack rats lived) just to see what they had collected over the years. I found silverware, string, rope and three sticks of dynamite which made me feel pretty uneasy. If dynamite sits long enough, it gets sensitive. Had the pack rat dropped a stick at the right angle, it would have blown all of us to Timbuktu. I carefully retrieved the three sticks and heaved them over the 2,000 foot east face. It didn't make a sound, but I sure felt safer. safer.

"Except for the pack rats, I didn't see animals around the lookout, not even bugs, although they got pretty fierce at Goat Flats. One guy, Eli B. Packer, working for the U.S. Coast and Geodetic Survey on a triangulation survey, hiked up to the cabin. He told me that the flies were driving his horse nuts. I told him that I hoped his horse was tied up and, when we hiked back to the Flats, sure enough, his horse had taken off. He was stuck with at least two-hundred pounds of gear. He was a tough guy, so the next morning he cut two poles, made a travois and piled his saddle and gear on it. The last I saw of him, he was heading across the Flats lugging the whole mess behind him. I heard later he made it all the way to Saddle Lake before he dropped the gear and took off after the horse. I don't think Eli enjoyed this area. He was from the South and in the register he had written, 'I'd rather be in Alabama'.

"Most days I had the place to myself. I'd get up early, brew myself a quart of coffee, dump in lots of sugar, some milk and sit back to watch the sunrise. Afterwards I'd begin my hourly calls and do some domestic chores; wash socks and clothes, refill the water supply. There was paint in the cabin and sometimes I'd touch up here and there. One day I had just finished a wall when a big bunch of flying ants crashed into the wall and plastered themselves on the fresh, sticky paint. Another time the northwest shutter blew off and the Forest Service dropped off some bolts and stuff at Goat Flats. I don't know why they did that. They could have brought it up to the lookout but they probably figured I needed the exercise. There was a government policy about keeping the windows so spotless you couldn't even make out the panes. I didn't work too hard at cleaning the windows. I really just wanted to look for fires.

"My first summer at the cabin a mosquito flew in the door. I don't know how he got there, but he was buzzing around bothering me, so I batted him against the window and there he stayed. When Charlie Thurston came up for inspection, he told me I should get rid of the mosquito. I must have forgotten because the next summer he came up and said, 'Harry, it seems like I saw that mosquito here last year.' He didn't go any further than that. I got the message.

"I also had lots of time to work on my cooking skills. On the good days I didn't try to cook any fancy dishes, but when the clouds rolled in, I'd make chili. It took an extra-long time to boil the kidney beans and it gave me an excuse to burn more kerosene. I'd also add some beef and lots of chili powder. It was pretty tasty. I also made stew, but I'm not sure how good that was. I served it to Charlie Thurston once and he told me he liked it, but when I offered seconds, he quickly said, 'No thanks'. Tasted good to me.

"I lived quite a bit on bread because it didn't weigh too much. To preserve it, I would wait until the first fair day which usually came before the loaves started to mold. Then I'd take the bread out of the packages and lay them out to dry. Sometimes my dinner was lots of bread and jam.

"You know, there weren't too many fires to report, although once I spotted thirty-five lightning fires. Since they were short-handed in Darrington, I was called down to fight fires. After a few days of that, I was anxious to get back to the lookout. I didn't like all that work.

"Some evenings I'd wake up and I could feel the electrical tension in the air. Occasionally my hair would frizzle a little because of the static electricity. A few times a summer we'd get some snow and ice at the lookout. Sometimes, when there were dark clouds hanging over the town and I was in the sunshine, I'd ring in and ask, 'What's the weather down there? It's drizzling sunshine up here'. They didn't think I was too funny.

"Visitors weren't common, mostly relatives, and I didn't miss them either. I think I had the first radio on Three Fingers. I could talk to the ranger station. The trouble was they could talk back to me, too. I had to call in every hour and I'd get tired of talking to people. At the time they were logging Green Mountain and that made plenty of noise. In the evenings I talked to other lookouts; some of our conversations were nonsensical. The people at headquarters didn't mind if you jabbered a bit as long as you didn't interfere with someone who had something important to say.

"One evening I made contact with a fire crew down on the ridge between Three Fingers and Squire Creek Pass. They were having steak for dinner and I felt I should check things out. I didn't have much time before evening check-in and the descent was fairly steep. But I was interested in steak. I scrambled down in no time, wolfed down some steak and grape juice and headed back to the cabin at a pretty good clip; too good I guess. Halfway to the cabin I lost my great meal. All that work, too!

"A number of times I ran over and climbed the north peak. I had to radio in every hour and I was able to make the round trip in forty minutes, dropping down the east side of the south peak on a manila rope, running up and over the middle peak and scrambling up the north. The chimney was sort of tricky but it wasn't too difficult. I was also able to go on some longer trips over to the Bullon area. I was young and full of pizzazz.

"In September the weather would turn, and you'd have to start shutting down. It was usually done in a downpour. The lookout had to take an inventory of everything in the cabin, but hardly anything except tools was packed down. I'd haul a load of equipment down to Goat Flats, but the office never seemed to send up a pack horse to haul it out. I'd head down the trail with as many tools as I could carry, drop them off at the end of the road and head back to the Flats, twenty-four miles in one day. After I'd gotten all of it to the end of the road, I'd treat myself to a toasted cheese sandwich.

"Nineteen forty-two was my last summer on Three Fingers. The Air Force called me and I had some interesting adventures. I flew a tour in Europe in heavy bombers. I was recalled to active duty during the Korean War and even flew some military cargo across "The Pond" during the Viet Nam conflict. During the war the Forest Service had a hard time finding young men to man the lookouts. In 'Forty-two there was a pacifist on Mt. Pugh. He used to tie up the radio horribly talking to fire camps or anyone with a radio. He lasted only a summer.

"In 1943 my mom served as the Three Fingers lookout. She brought my three younger brothers because my father was working in a Seattle shipyard at the time. She was on the mountain, not so much for fire protection, but rather to watch for Japanese planes or incendiary balloons. The government was afraid the Japanese might launch a bomber task force and sneak into Puget Sound via the Cascades. They had a whole network of people watching.

"The whole bunch lived in a big tent at the Flats (the cabin was not manned). It wasn't very comfortable but my brothers really liked living there. They got to roam around. Harold Engles showed them how to make a sled and they'd get on and slide down a snow slope into a pond just below the Flats. The kids got a kick out of that.

"One day the packer let Tommy ride Mabel and she bucked him off. He hit his head a wallop and was knocked out colder than a cucumber for about fifteen minutes. Another time he got real homesick, like little kids will, and he hiked all the way back to Tuckerville, over fifteen miles. Tommy lived at the farm for a few day until he got lonesome for the family, so he hiked back to Goat Flats. He was eight at the time and my mom was real impressed with him. We all were used to living that way all our lives and generally knew what was dangerous and what wasn't. My mother worried a lot but didn't try to tie us down.

"The lookout wasn't manned after 1943. Funny, considering all the trouble the Forest Service went to getting it built. After the war I went back to the forests but not the Forest Service. I set chokers for loggers, worked for the National Park Service at Mt. Rainier and finished school at the University of Washington. I met Eileen at the University of Washington. She liked the mountains too. In July of 1949, she and I climbed Little Tahoma. Eileen must have been giddy from the altitude (it was over 11,000 feet on the summit) because she proposed to me. I took advantage of the situation and accepted. The next day she bought both rings and we were married that evening.

"I found a job in West Virginia, but we didn't like it there because the mountains weren't high enough. I managed to get transferred to Salt Lake City and when I got home after the Korean War, I didn't want to stay there either. I wanted to be in the Northwest.

"The mountains have always been a special place for the Tuckers. Counting the relatives, forty-four, all but about five or six of the Tucker clan have climbed Three Fingers. That number doesn't include some of the Tucker dogs who have also made the trip. We hauled our kids up when they were young, Pat when she was four. We even took Eileen's mother up. She didn't have much experience in the mountains, but she did real well. I've climbed Three Fingers over twenty times, from the Boulder River, up the Mountaineers' trail, from Saddle Creek and Meadow Mountain. I even have a lake named after me; one of those small ones between Three Fingers and Bullon. The man who put together the book, *"Lakes of Western Washington"*, was working next door to my brother's office in Olympia. He was interested in all those unnamed lakes between Three Fingers and Whitehorse and asked my brother, 'Jim, do these lakes have any names?'

"Jim says, 'No, I don't know, but my brother, Harry, has been there a couple of times.'

"The guy said, 'We'll name one of them Tucker Lake.'

"Now, I don't know how legal that is but it's a nice touch.

"In 1972 we got a bunch of people together to make repairs on the cabin. We almost lost Kenn Carpenter's daughter out one of the windows. In 1978, when we climbed Three Fingers, Goat Flats was as clean as I'd seen it in years, but the cabin was in poor condition. Someone either left the shutters up or didn't fasten them securely on the northwest and southeast sides and they blew off. I wrote a few letters (I'm pretty good at that), the Forest Service supplied the materials, and volunteers fixed things up. With a little loving care, the lookout will last a long time.

"Nineteen seventy-eight was my last year on the mountain. I got in a bicycle accident which bunged me up pretty badly. I'd really get moving down this hill in Bellingham. A policeman stopped me once and gave me a warning for speeding. He was smiling and I suspect I was set up. Well, that accident pretty much curtailed my climbing but I kept up my interest. I wrote a bunch of letters in support of the Boulder River Wilderness. There are some areas I wanted to see preserved, but the Forest Service has this screwy idea that if an area has been logged or touched by a road, it will never again be wilderness. Heck, the trees will grow back and the roads will disappear. I don't think I'll ever lose my interest in that mountain.

"My summers in the lookout were vacation with pay and, besides, I liked the mountains anyway. Heck, the Forest Service took $5 for staying in that lookout, but I still thought I was pretty lucky. Where else can you sit on your front step and watch the ferries steaming across Puget Sound as the sun sets over the Olympics, spot all five of the Washington volcanoes or watch a barn dance going on in Darrington? No, I never felt any hurry to get back to the asphalt jungle. For me there was no better place to be."

Harry Tucker reads the *Seattle Times*, 1942.

Mt. Pugh lookout, August 1929. Left to right, Stella Mills,
Edith Bedal, Jean Bedal and Otto Dikes.

CHAPTER NINE
Looking all around for a route up

There comes a time when the older climber steps off the trail to let the younger climber pass by. It is not always a graceful transition. The older climber sometimes clings tenaciously to the youthful notions of invulnerabilty and immortality, while the body, tired and aching, makes a mockery of them. The young climber's legs never ache. The lungs never lack for air. The back carries the heaviest pack. The young climber looks for the unclimbed summit, the hardest peak and when he stands triumphantly on top, he reaches even higher, as the older climber once did.

In 1932 Art Winder was as good as a climber could get. He and his buddies, Forest Farr and Norval Grigg literally dragged John Lehmann up the north peak of Three Fingers, the peak he had dreamed of climbing for years. And they considered it a lark. Sixteen years earlier Lehmann had pushed on to the summit of Rainier when the the leader of the climb, Major E.S. Ingraham, then almost 70, decided that poor weather would keep the party from making the top. In 1946, a back injury curtailed Winder's mountain adventures. He could only look at the steep north ridge of Three Fingers that Kenn Carpenter would climb twelve years later.

The aging climber slowly accepts the fact of mortality and his goals change accordingly. The youthful compulsion to push the limits and to be first to the top are eclipsed by a simple desire to be in the mountains where time slows to a crawl and death's stillness in the fall is followed by glorious rebirth in the summer. At that age it is a pleasure to step aside when young climbers charge up the trail.

Art Winder several years ago was denied even the pleasure of getting out into the mountains. Struck down by Lou Gehrig's disease, he has watched as the body begins to disobey even the simplest commands from the brain. Five years ago Winder, in his late seventies, was quite active. He still got out into the mountains and worked hard in his garden. The disease first took root in his vocal chords and eventually robbed him of his voice. But he continued to lead as normal a life as possible.

The disease moved inexorably to the rest of his body, and before my first meeting with Art Winder, I was unsure of what to expect. I was surprised to find a man who sat erect, loved to laugh and still had a sparkle in his eye. I spent the morning reminiscing with Art, his wife, Ov, and Gertrude Shorrock. We had a lively conversation. Art had pen and paper at hand and would scribble answers to questions almost as quickly as I asked.

I visited a month later and, after lunch, Art, Ov and I retired to the TV to watch the University of Washington basketball team take on UCLA. The Winders are avid Husky fans. Using eyes, hands and written notes, Art kept up a running commentary on the game. It was apparent that he had refused to give in to the debilitating disease. The challenges were different, more elemental, but he seemed to have chosen to face them head on, much as he might have on Mount Goode, Big Four or Three Fingers. Fifty-four years ago the challenge for Art Winder had been to scale unclimbed peaks. Today it is to keep intact spirit and dignity. Who is to say which is the more difficult challenge?

****

In December of 1986, Art Winder died. He had asked that the Mountaineers' *Good Night Song* be sung at his memorial service. The tune which he had sung with friends around many a mountain campfire, concluded with the words:

> *Good night, we must part,*
> *God keep watch o'er us all,*
> *where we go,*
> *Till we meet once again,*
> *Good Night.*

****

Viewed from farmland along the Snohomish River delta between Everett and Marysville, Mt. Three Fingers demands attention. The sun on its slopes marks the advance of the day; its dark, castellated summits framed in a corona of the sun's first light and awash with the full spectrum of reds at twilight. Roiling thunderheads butt up against it in the east and billow ominously upward. Its three peaks floating above a sea of valley fog give assurances of a fair day. Whether basking in an azure sky or partially obscured by mist, Three Fingers is a center of attention on the ragged Cascade skyline stretching from Mt. Baker to Rainier.

From the forks of the Stillaguamish River, which parallel on the north and south, Three Fingers is less easily observed; an occasional view from the Mountain Loop Highway. From one side it entices the eye while from other sides it appears remote and mysterious. John Lehmann, an Everett mountaineer, had seen the mountain from all aspects. He was drawn to Three Fingers but wanted more than valley views. He wanted to stand atop its highest summit, the north peak.

By 1931 Three Fingers remained the only major unclimbed peak on the Cascade's western crest. For ten years Lehmann, often accompanied by his brother, Chris, had made several attempts to climb Three Fingers. According to Art, "Those two covered the whole countryside around Three Fingers from all directions except the one that was the logical approach. John was real anxious to make the climb. It had become a major goal for him."

Lehmann was a conservative climber but his sense of caution didn't save him from some nervous moments in the mountains. He had spent two very cold and wet nights on the summit of Mt. Rainier, after ascending the volcano with the intention of setting off fireworks for Renton's 4th of July celebration. The display was a success but during the night a storm moved in covering their blankets with several inches of snow. It was a wet and miserable group of pyrotechnic mountaineers who stumbled down the Emmons Glacier two days later.

More often than not, Lehmann's outings were planned to take into account any eventuality. He kept a complete record of his climbs detailing what he had done, when, with whom and in what kind of weather.

Winder says, "We'd be on a trip and come to a large rock, for example. John would whip out a notebook and announce that two years before we had reached the same point two minutes earlier!"

Winder remembers him as a tall, strong, stern man, not too emotional but possessing a sense of humor "rarely let out for public exposure. He and Chris had a steady pace which made you lose your breath uphill, but coming down, we had to wait for them."

The "logical" approach to Three Fingers became more evident after Engles' and Bedal's 1929 reconnaissance of the south peak. A new trail led to Tin Can Gap but, as yet, no successful climbs of the North Peak had been recorded. Lehmann planned a climb of Three Fingers for the 4th of July weekend in 1931 and he called Art Winder to see if he could get people "to make a determined assault on the peak."

"John was thinking of several days with bivouacs but the rest of us kind of perplexed him because the climb turned out to be easier."

Winder and partners, Forest Farr and Norval Grigg, were of a different generation of climbers. Although having climbed seriously for only a few years, they had already made several impressive first ascents in the Cascades, including the first recorded ascent of Big Four. For them time was of the essence. A weekend climb was usually a sprint from start to finish. Leaving jobs on noon Saturday, the young climbers would race up bumpy dirt roads, race up the trails, bag a peak and race home, often returning with just enough time to clean up for work on Monday morning. By 1931 Winder and Farr were, according to Grigg, two of the best natural climbers in the Northwest.

Art was a tall, wiry man, often wearing a knowing smile and was the catalyst for many serious climbs. Gertrude Shorrock, a long time member of the Mountaineers, remembers Art as a strong leader who "led the first climb I was ever on. It was a snow climb in early spring up Denny Peak. We had a big party and at a steep place on the way down, one girl slipped and was instantly out of control, sliding down a long slope with a rock slide below. Art's reaction was instantaneous and he stopped her before she reached the rocks. He became a hero, at least to us beginners. Art was a lovable person, not really outgoing, but aware of other people's needs. He was very kind to those who weren't as good."

Winder possessed a real zest for adventure and trying new things. "When Herb Stranberg and I learned how to rappel, we wanted to show it off at the weekly Mountaineers' campfire. We ran up the bank above the fire and looped the rope around a tree. I headed down first, swinging out over an overhang when part of the bank collapsed showering me and the people below with dirt and rocks. I found myself hanging upside down but at least was able to demonstrate the effectiveness of the technique, I think."

Grigg was a high school buddy of Winder's, living only a few blocks from the Winder home in Seattle. Walks home from school extended to hikes around the Puget Sound area on weekends, sometimes even to the mountains. Grigg spent two summers working for the Forest Service at Silverton beginning in 1926. That same year both joined the Seattle Mountaineers. Winder said of Grigg, "Norval was several inches shorter than I but, as the term goes, was split up the middle and had a longer stride than I. He enjoyed fine things, from food to equipment. When you camped with "Jiggs", you ate better than you otherwise would. He always had the best and latest equipment and he was our unofficial photographer on the trips.

"Forry was a gem, good looking, in excellent physical shape, very honest, funny and supportive. He was well-versed in the out-of-doors and his pan bread was a basic necessity on our expeditions. I still relish the compliment he gave me when we were discussing possibilities for a successful climb. I asked his

Norval Grigg, left, and Art Winder.

First ascent of north peak. Victorious party descends from the col.

opinion and he said, 'You lead. I'll follow.' If I were to pick a best friend, it would be Forry."

The morning of the 4th, after unloading their gear from Grigg's 1930 Model A Ford, the group left the Boulder River trailhead and before noon had covered the ten miles to Goat Flats. "When we reached Goat Flats, John wanted to camp, but we decided to go farther and scout Tin Can Gap. At the gap John again said, 'Let's get our packs and bivouac here.' But we persuaded him to traverse the glacier and see what the climb looked like up close."

The quartet easily crossed the Three Fingers glacier to the col between the north and middle fingers. They were left with no more than 250 feet of rock climbing. Grigg scrambled up the Middle Peak.

"I was feeling energetic and romped up. There was a Prince Albert can with some strips of paper which had about fifteen names written on them. From the middle peak, the north looked absolutely sheer, impossible. But of course it wasn't."

At the col Winder remembers Lehmann "scurrying about looking for a bivouac. He still had it in his mind to spend the night. Meanwhile Forry and I discovered a way across the face and decided to give it a go. We put on our tennis shoes and scampered across the glacier to an overhanging chimney."

Grigg watched as Winder and Farr rather easily stemmed what looked to him to be a formidable chimney. "They cleaned out the chimney yelling, 'look out below' as they dumped maybe a bushel basket of rocks, not many."

The two emerged from the chimney and called down that the rest of the climb was an easy scramble. "Forry and I had to traverse diagonally a steep and smooth rock face with rather small hand and foot holds. From here we swung into the chimney. It was short and not too difficult, although it was eerie to look down between your legs and see nothing but snow on the glacier below."

Lehmann was given the honor of leading the last section and standing first on the summit. It was 6:30 p.m. From the north peak the climbers could see the south peak, which would soon lose fifteen feet off its top to make room for the lookout cabin. The day was brilliant. The Puget Sound basin, often hidden in clouds of coal smoke, shimmered in the distance. "It was a magnificent day," said Grigg. "We wanted to stay longer."

Art Winder, left, and Forest Farr.

Unfortunately they had little time on top to savor either their accomplishment or the sun. A large, cigar-shaped cloud materialized and engulfed the north peak. Fearing a storm and wondering if Lehmann had been right about a bivouac, the foursome retreated, only to find, once they reached the glacier, that the only cloud on the horizon hung over the north peak.

The happy, but tired, alpinists reached camp after dark and spent a comfortable evening watching fireworks extravaganzas from Olympia to Victoria. Grigg remembers Everett having a "particularly nice display". No restaurant ever had a finer view. According to Forest Farr, "Norval prepared dinner while Art and I did most of the flunky work, pitching the tent, getting wood. Norval took great pride in preparing our meals. On this evening he had carefully cooked up a dish of canned chicken breast and rice. A brisk wind had come up and Norval was bent over very close to the boiling water because the wind was blowing the salt away every time he tried to drop it in. After serving each of us a heaping plateful of the savory dish, he served himself. I can still see Norval sitting there with his plate on his knee and his spoon in his hand. After taking a judicious taste, he asked John Lehmann, 'How do you like it?'

"John replied rather seriously, 'I think it has too much chicken in it.' The shocked look on Grigg's face, after John's remark, caused Art and me to break up and proved one of the highlights of the trip for me."

Unlike his experience on Rainier 16 years before, Lehmann awoke to sun on the Fifth of July but his sleep may have been just as uncomfortable. To save weight, he had brought a double sleeping bag. Lehmann and Winder fit very tightly and both spent a miserable night unable to turn without awakening the other. According to Grigg, "John would have liked to spend more time at the Flats, but we were in a bit of a hurry. We packed up early, hiked to the car, drove John to Everett and spent the night at Snoqualmie Lodge, near the pass."

Winder commented, "I think John was stunned that it had gone so easily after all those years of trying."

Farr said of the climb, "It was a very amusing trip as far as I was concerned. I got a real laugh out of it. I think, on most first ascents, the climbers bring home hair-raising tales of difficulty, but Three Fingers was almost like a pushover. It was very simple from a mountaineering standpoint although route finding and accessibility were concerns."

Winder was impressed by the tranquillity, the verdant meadows and brightly colored wildflowers. He wrote about the mountain in the 1931 Mountaineer Annual calling it, "the most beautiful climb in the West Cascades".

A year later Winder, Farr and Grigg returned to Three Fingers as leaders of an Everett Mountaineers climb, but they got no farther than Tupso Pass where strong winds and rain kept them tent-bound. After the first night, most of the "one-hundred" climbers headed for home. The flooding Boulder had made it impossible for the pack string to reach the camp. After a miserable second night, the remaining climbers headed for home. The only climber not disappointed was the cook, who had expected a pack-string worth of food for the second day's meals. It was a monumental task keeping those wet and hungry climbers happy.

After the first ascent Three Fingers became a popular climb for the Mountaineers. In 1932, Lehmann, along with Stew Hertz, Kenneth Chapman and Bernard Crain placed the first register on the north peak. Chapman, a retired chemical engineer for Weyerhauser and longtime member of the Everett Mountaineers, remembers meeting Harry Bedal on the trail. Bedal was stringing telephone wire for the lookout. The trio had just come from a climb of Sloan Peak and Bedal laughed a little and said, "Sloan is such an easy climb. You could take your mother up in a wheelbarrow."

Except for Lehmann, none of the first ascent party ever returned to the summit of Three Fingers. In the late 1940's, Winder, who had been grounded by a back injury incurred while swimming, drove up Squire Creek to take a look at the back side of Three Fingers, but due to the angle of the sun, the north ridge was hidden by shadows. Winder couldn't make out any detail, but he did say, "It looked formidable."

Left to right, Norval Grigg, Lloyd Anderson and Art Winder on summit of Mt. St. Helens, 1935.

CHAPTER TEN

Bushwhacking is His Specialty

The bookcase in Kenn Carpenter's living room is filled with books on mountaineering. Many of the books are alpine guides, including Fred Beckey's earliest guides to climbing in the Cascades. In the Fifties and Sixties, Carpenter was the leader of many first ascents in the Darrington and Verlot area. He had also made several attempts on Mount McKinley. Along the way Carpenter acquired the reputation as a "Bushwhacker Par Excellence".

Ron Miller, a companion on many of Carpenter's wilder climbs, says the title is a perfect fit. "One night, several years ago, Kenn and I were making our way off Sloan Peak in the dark. We had a map and flashlight, but it was cloudy and we really couldn't see a thing. It was vital that we get to a tiny notch on the ridge. Periodically Kenn would check the map and then give out a yodel. He'd wait for the echo, count the number of seconds and calculate our exact position. At one point, and we still couldn't see a thing, Kenn told me to walk fifty feet straight ahead. I counted off the steps, took a look around with the flashlight and found that we had hit the notch dead center. He could calculate position like almost nobody else. That wasn't the only time either.

"We got caught in another whiteout, this time in Alaska. After hiking on this glacier all day, Ken announced, 'Okay, this is where we're going to camp.' We spent two days in that camp waiting out a storm and when the fog cleared, we found that we couldn't have camped anywhere else. One hundred feet to the right and we would have been heading up a steep slope. Fifty feet in the other direction and the glacier dropped off precipitously. Ken is probably the only men I've ever heard of who bushwhacked off a climb of Mount Rainier. But I've been told he had to go out of his way to find it."

It takes a leap of imagination to envision the middle-aged, bespectacled man who sits across the room from me, shouldering a huge pack and gleefully crashing through jungles of Devil's

Club and slide alder with wild abandon. But a sly smile and chuckle at the mention of the word "bushwhacking" indicate that he relishes the thought of taking the road less traveled.

For several years a back injury has kept Carpenter from carrying heavy loads and has limited his activity in the mountains to day hikes. About six years ago Carpenter took up running. A middle-of-the-pack runner, Carpenter has nonetheless approached the sport with the same enthusiasm he gave his climbing. He has completed several marathons, but not content with the 26.2-mile race, he has stepped up to fifty-mile races. Carpenter chose as his first run at that distance, a race in the foothills of the Cascades near Bellingham; not only fifty miles but hilly to boot. It seems that Kenn Carpenter will never get over his zest for doing things a little differently.

****

Kenn Carpenter moved from Pennsylvania to Everett in the fall of 1953. A weekend hiker in the Appalachians, he was awed and intrigued by the rugged, snow-capped Cascades.

"I joined the Everett Mountaineers and decided to take the basic mountaineering course. At the time Everett didn't conduct climbing classes. I thought, 'Why not do it ourselves?' Others in Everett thought it a great idea and elected me, a nonclimber, chairman. We delayed the course for six weeks while I took Seattle's course and field trips. With help from a few Seattle instructors and notes I had taken, we put together our first course that spring."

The number of climbs recorded in Carpenter's log grew dramatically after 1953. He counted almost thirty in 1958, the year he first climbed the north ridge of Three Fingers. The route description in Fred Beckey's guide book was sketchy but looked interesting. Although Beckey had climbed it, Carpenter and climbing buddy, Jerry Cate, figured there might be a second ascent for them. A third member, Ron Muecke, was added on Cate's recommendation. He had watched Muecke almost run up the summit pyramid on Mt. Olympus and was impressed.

On a Saturday morning in July, the trio parked at the end of the Squire Creek road and bushwhacked up an ever-narrowing timbered ridge until they reached the basin connecting Three Fingers and Whitehorse. In 1956 two Army jet trainers, returning home to Paine Field after circling Glacier Peak, had flown into a cloud near the ridge and crashed twenty-five feet below the crest. The climbers found wreckage strewn across the snow, a sobering sight. In the late afternoon they camped near Craig Lakes, caught enough fish for dinner and that evening spotted fifteen mountain goats at the base of the North Ridge.

From the northeast, the north ridge of Three Fingers appears as a dark multi-tiered pillar with a broad, gently sloping snow field separating the steep, exposed lower rock rib from the summit spire. On one side is the fearsome east face and on the other a glacier hanging precipitously over Craig Lakes.

The climbing the next morning was, according to Carpenter, "exposed but not difficult. That changed when we reached a bench five to eight feet wide and about fifteen feet long. We looked up a sixty-foot slab rising at a forty-five degree angle; no problem except that it was moss-covered and water was running down its face. We roped up and I was able to climb thirty feet and place a piton before being forced down to the ledge. I was numb, blue almost, and soaking wet. I had left the piton in and asked for volunteers. Ron said he'd like to give a try.

"He got just as wet and cold but he managed to reach a ledge and belay me up. The rest of the climb was lovely class four climbing up the north pinnacle, rough rock but solid with lots of hand holds. On top, as we were taking in some sun and food, Ron admitted rather sheepishly, 'I didn't want to tell you guys this, but that was my first roped rock climb ever.' Jerry looked at me and burst out laughing.

"We decided we weren't going to retrace our steps but rather descend the standard route, which would leave us miles from the car. We figured we could hitch a ride.

"It was four o'clock when we started down and, with several miles left to the road, the sun went down leaving us in the dark. None of us had hiked the trail before. By one in the morning we were still on the trail somewhere below Saddle Lake. We'd hike some, snooze for a few minutes and hike some more. At one point we spotted some red, blinking lights and thought we were near the trailhead. They were only one-hundred yards away but, as we hiked, the lights continued to remain just beyond our reach and then disappeared. We later found they were the lights from the Jim Creek Naval Station several miles away. It was a bit strange. We were exhausted and finally dropped on the trail but the cold hurt so that we decided to keep on moving.

"At dawn we reached the road and stopped at the first house in order to call home because we were overdue. The lady looked at us strangely and would only let one of us in to call. We must have looked a bit grungy. We managed to thumb a ride to the Darrington Ranger Station where the ranger bawled us out for not registering for the climb although eventually he got us a ride back to the car. We drove home and went to work, which was typical of many of my climbs; climb all weekend, get home in time to shower and head for the job."

It wasn't until after climbing another route sketchily detailed by Beckey (this one on Whitehorse), that Carpenter ran into the author and quizzed him about the first ascents that he assumed Beckey had made. "Beckey explained to me that he'd never made those climbs. He just thought they looked good and he had made some educated guesses about the route description. We were the first after all."

In the early 1960's Carpenter, along with Bob Briggs, Paul Bergman and Don Johnson, made a first ascent of the west arete of Three Fingers. The climbers spent the first night comfortably ensconced on a grassy ledge 500 feet below the summit. They heated a sumptuous meal of pre-cooked chicken and hamburger and later in the evening, using flashlights, communicated in morse code with a group camped at Goat Flats.

Carpenter remembers, "The last five-hundred feet were the steepest and on the first lead I climbed around a corner where the ridge reared up at an eighty-degree angle. The rock was fractured. I continued to the last good belay spot and from there Briggs led. The rock was still awful and he was unable to put in any protection. If he fell he died, but he didn't and past that section the route to the summit was enjoyable." On that occasion the group returned to their cars well before dark.

****

The broad and sheer 2,000-foot east face of Three Fingers would seem to offer numerous climbing challenges, but it has over the years received scant attention from elite alpinists. The rock is somewhat less than trustworthy; seemingly solid hand and footholds may shatter and spray the air with potential brain busters. Experienced climbers have surveyed the mountain's east face, considering it for possible routes and determined that there were far less risky ways to get one's name in a guidebook.

Three Fingers' attraction lies in its shorter, less technical routes. They offer more than enough challenge for the climber of moderate skills. There is a bit of roped rock climbing and some steep snow to cross. For some mountain climbers or scramblers, it is their McKinley or Rainier.

****

One evening, while relaxing at home, Kenn Carpenter received a phone call from Washington, D.C. "A man was interested in climbing Three Fingers and asked if I would be his guide. It seems he'd wanted to climb the mountain ever since his college days at the University of Washington.

"I was a bit hesitant, but he assured me that at 52, he was in good shape and was willing to get into even better shape. I agreed and told him I'd send him info on equipment and exercise. He came out later in the summer and we had an enjoyable climb. I brought along a couple of friends and we taught Sam how to belay right on the mountain. I could tell he was nervous and it was all he could do to step off the trail onto the snow, but you had to give Sam credit. I never charged him.

"Sam was a fascinating guy, but even after the climb, I didn't feel like I knew him. He didn't tell me much about himself and I didn't ask. He was really interested in the mountains and conservation.

"The next summer we got together for a climb of Glacier Peak. Sam wanted to stop at the ranger station before the climb. He seemed to know a great deal about budgetary matters and, in fact, gave a discourse on the subject. The same thing happened when we ran into the ranger at Kennedy Hot Springs. I was beginning to wonder, 'How does this guy know all these things?

"The next morning, shortly after leaving our camp, we reached the glacier. As we put on our crampons and roped up, I noticed that Sam was getting real nervous. Suddenly he turned to me and said, 'Ken, we've got to have a talk. If anything happens to me, there will be hell to pay in the government.'

"Now, I found that statement rather interesting and I started asking questions. It seemed that "old" Sam was second in command at the Bureau of the Budget. He was out west that summer, 1966, studying the proposal for the North Cascades National Park. Secretary of Agriculture, Orville Freeman, and Secretary of the Interior, Stewart Udall, were coming out a week later and Sam was coordinating the trip. We made the summit, had a grand time, but I was extra careful. Sam certainly enjoyed the mountains, especially Three Fingers. He came out another summer and hiked to Goat Flats by himself."

Sam was Phillip S. Hughes. Hughes had grown up in Olympia and, while attending the University of Washington, spent a great deal of time staring at Three Fingers from his apartment window. Hughes recalls, "Three Fingers was somewhat less imposing than the biggies, but I was never a climber in the rock sense. The mountain appealed to me. I had hiked to Tin Can Gap in the late 1930's and managed to reach the ladders below the cabin in the middle 1950's, but I wanted to climb the north peak. While working for the Bureau of the Budget in the 1960's, my interest and first-hand knowledge of the North Cascades came in handy. I mediated the discussions between Henry Jackson, Orville Freeman and Stewart Udall while they wrangled over use of the lands designated for park and wilderness status.

"I got Kenn's name from the ranger at Gold Bar and we made a date over the phone. When I showed up at his house, there were two other younger men. At the beginning of the hike, those young guys set quite a pace. We raced up this extremely steep trail, virtually no switchbacks. It was quite a trip. We had gorgeous weather at the Flats, the best I have ever seen in the Cascades. We had views of all the volcanos, including Mount Hood. We climbed the mountain the next morning and hiked out. I hurt like hell going down. Boy, was I beat, but it was worth it. I would certainly like to visit Goat Flats again. I just might do it."

****

In July of 1940, Fred Noble and Robert Lee, 16 and 17-year-olds from Bellingham, climbed to the cabin and signed the register. Bob Craig, who was manning the lookout that summer, remembers Noble as "an intelligent, athletic teenager, pursuing a new love. He had just discovered the mountains. His ice axe was new, his nailed boots still had every Tricouni intact. He had everything but experience and the judgement it brings."

According to a report in the Bellingham Herald, "Craig, who had left his post on Three Fingers to go to a cache at the glacier, encountered the boys on the glacier. Craig undertook to guide them across the glacier. Encountering a steep declivity, Craig stationed the boys on the top while he went to the base of the slope to remove his pack so that he might return and assist the hikers. It was while he was removing the pack that he heard the Noble boy fall, but before the lookout could render aid, the boy shot by him and crashed into the rocks."

Bob Craig said, "He tried to glissade a slope that he should not have and hit the one rock in the whole snow field. He was unconscious when I reached him and died several hours later in Tin Can Gap. Harland Eastwood came up that night with a crew of CCC and a pack string to take him out."

Eastwood remembers, "Bob Craig had managed to get him off the glacier and up to Tin Can Gap. This doctor in Darrington had given some medicine for him, but when we got there and felt his pulse, we knew he was dead. The job ahead was getting him down. There were only four of us and we had a horrible time getting down. The narrow trail and rock slide above Goat Flats made it almost impossible. We would go about a block or so and have to let him down. When we got down to Tupso Pass, we were able to put him on a horse. I just laid him gently on a mattress, put a blanket around him, then took a rope and tied the two ends underneath kind of like a cinch. His mother and father were very nice to me for a long period of time. They would come up and spend time with me."

Thirty-six years later Three Fingers was the scene of another climbing death. Dr. Leland Rice, climbing alone, inexplicably headed left on the ridge above Goat Flats instead of following the trail which winds around to the right. He fell into the basin which drains the Boulder River, a drop of seven-hundred feet. Dave Cameron and a friend saw Rice fall but could not reach him. They hiked out and called Snohomish County Search and Rescue. A group of seven Explorer Scouts led by Doug Shaw found Rice in a small crevasse. He died at about 7:30 p.m. and Shaw remembers that at almost exactly the moment Rice was declared dead, it started raining hard and didn't let up for a couple of days. It was, according to Shaw, very weird.

The Everett Mountain Rescue team arrived and helped retrieve the body from the crevasse. The rain was torrential and the Scouts who were bringing the body back were completely exhausted by the time they reached the flats and the relative comfort of the shelter. Some members of a back-up group, holed up at the Saddle Lake shelter, suffered from mild hypothermia.

****

In the early 1960's the approach to the mountain was shortened by six miles thanks to a logging road which snaked in from the south around Green and Meadow Mountains all the way to Tupso Pass. From Canyon Creek, climbers found an even shorter, more direct route to the high country, although Kenn Carpenter remarked that it saved time if one was in good shape. Otherwise there was a lot of "huffin' and puffin.''

The number of ascents of both north and south peaks tripled, and by the early 1970's an average of eighty people were climbing to the lookout each summer. The trail which as late as 1970 had grass growing in it, began to lose its pristine beauty. It became rutted and meandered muddily through some of the meadows. Campsites were stripped of grass and reduced to patches of dirt and fire scars. It became hard to imagine a time when Goat Flats hadn't been overused. There are few hints of the brand new trail that Lehmann, Grigg, Winder and Farr hiked on that 4th of July weekend in 1931, although occasionally one finds a patch of pink phlox pushing through the dirt in the middle of the trail, grass spilling over both sides to hide the path which disappears in the snow above Tin Can Gap. Sometimes the lucky climber will even spot a goat. There are rare moments on the mountain when the climber feels as if he is the first to climb Three Fingers and if gray clouds cover the sun and he is tired and the north peak looks distant, the climber, like John Lehmann, may start looking for a bivouac site.

CHAPTER ELEVEN
A New Coat of Paint

Just another Three Fingers climb, but I am a bit too frazzled to feel anything but relief. My cousin, Theresa, standing on top of her first mountain, watches in awed silence as the sun disappears beneath the clouds which cover all but the highest peaks. An hour ago I wasn't sure where we'd be when the sun set. Theresa knows nothing of this, which is fine with me. I was the guide. I was supposed to know everything, but the mountain which I assumed I knew, dare I say, like the back of my hand, has disabused me of that conceit at every turn in the trail.

Snow covered the route from car to cabin, my first surprise, and Theresa and I spent most of the time floundering somewhere north or south of the trail. Theresa was exhausted by the time we reached Goat Flats and showed signs of hypothermia. Hot soup and warm clothing solved that problem, but I was nervous about our chances of reaching the cabin. I didn't want to push Theresa, but it was the best place to be when darkness came. Thus far almost everything I seemed to know about the mountain was covered by snow. After kicking steps in the crusty snow all the way to Tin Can Gap, I found that all else familiar was concealed by fog. I felt blind on a mountain I thought I could climb with my eyes closed.

After roping up, the two of us groped (only I knew we were groping) across the crevassed snow field in search of the gap which would reunite us with the last section of trail. Without landmarks I relied on intuition, but I didn't trust it. The traverse was interminable and I was fast losing the confident facade of the alpine guide. Suddenly, almost magically, the clouds parted to reveal the cabin looming almost 500 feet directly above us. We were halfway between the col separating the north and middle peaks. I felt like a little blindfolded kid who'd been spun around and pinned the tail on the donkey's ear. At least I knew where we were and I knew where to go. Familiar sights appeared in the fog, and I felt giddy, as though I should start humming

"Amazing Grace". Instead I turned our rope team around and headed for the cabin.

Theresa and I were too tired to do much cheering when we reached the cabin. After dinner, Theresa read through the register and afterwards wrote a few sentences of her own, words that would always be there to remind her of this time whenever she returned to the cabin.

I flopped down onto the bed, amazed at the joy I felt. I had never been so happy to be in the cabin, but while reading through the register I found that perhaps I had been mistaken. Each of my previous entries had been rather cliched paeans to the climb and cabin. The experiences, the person, different, but the emotions carbon copies. I had to admit that every climb had been special. After a day spent struggling to remember, I was content to lay back and let the remembering wash over me.

We leave more on a mountain than footprints. Bits and pieces of who we once were are scattered along the trail. Ground into the dirt by hikers who follow, muddied and buried beneath winter snows, those memories spring at us from the trail whenever we return. Change on a mountain is imperceptible to the human eye. Unlike the old neighborhood, old homes or friends, the mountain remains untouched by the passage of time. Those of us who are not writers or photographers have difficulty protecting our personal history from the revisionism and plain forgetfulness of the mind. Moments that make our present are evanescent, too often dancing from the grasp into the dark disappearing of the past.

The mountain preserves memory for us. A switchback, a creek crossing, a boulder, snowfield, all spark memory that is luminous, fresh and only slightly gilded by romance. The trail up Three Fingers is like a personal time-line charting my progress through adolescence to adulthood. And each time I open the door to the lookout cabin, my memories are given flesh and bone.

Sitting in the cabin I am reintroduced to all the people I have been, at times terrified, cocky, silly, serious, pompous and reflective. The register offers palpable reminders and I have often been tempted to erase or alter some of the more embarrassing inscriptions (my, I was verbose and "terribly" funny), but I don't. It wouldn't be fair. It wouldn't be true.

The cabin serves a similar purpose for the hundreds of climbers who have returned to the south peak over the past fifty years. Harry Tucker spent much of his youth on the mountain. He shared adventures on the peak with friends and most of the Tucker clan. When he married Eileen, he brought her to the cabin. As soon as his children were old enough to walk, he brought them and I imagine he hoped someday to bring his grandchildren. There was a lifetime of memories preserved in that cabin.

Harry was vigilant when it came to maintaining the cabin. He volunteered his time, and when he was no longer able to climb the mountain, he wrote letters and kept people informed of the cabin's condition. Harry knew better than anyone else that when the lookout cabin collapsed, memory would die in its ruins.

****

In the fall of 1942, as Harry Tucker bolted the door and windows on the Three Fingers cabin, he gave little thought to who might man the lookout in 1943. He probably would have been surprised and a bit disappointed to know that he would be the last. After only eight years of service, the cabin, which had kept Forest Service construction crews busy for the better part of two summers, was abandoned. According to Harold Engles, "We just didn't have enough qualified men because of the war. I sent Mrs. Tucker to Goat Flats in 1943 and just let the office think she was on the peak. She had her children with her and I was worried about those little Tuckers running around the lookout. They had enough adventures at Goat Flats. After that we just kept the lookout closed.

"The Forest Service continued to build new lookouts even into the early 1950's, but after the War things began to change. There seemed to be more jobs for the men returning from service. The young men we had been able to count on in the past were finding better paying jobs. There was more emphasis put on aerial detection. I'd done some of that in the early 1920's, but after the war there was a surplus of planes, much better than those we'd used in the past. Radios also made fire detection easier. There were more logging roads in the mountains. And there was the cost to consider."

The cost of building and maintaining a fire lookout had tripled since the 1930's when the Forest Service relied heavily on the CCC's. Engles remained, until his retirement, a strong supporter of the lookout system. "If it had been my decision, I wouldn't have phased out the lookouts. I always felt a little more secure knowing there were competent men watching the forests."

Twenty years after Three Fingers was closed, the number of manned lookouts in the Darrington District had dwindled to three: Miner's Ridge, Green and North Mountains. Higgins, which had been locked up for years, collapsed. Vandals burned the lookout on Huckleberry Mountain and the Forest Service did the burning on Mount Pugh.

In 1965 Congress passed an act which made it easier for citizens to sue a government agency for injuries suffered on government property, through no fault of the victim. Harry Tucker worried about the fate of his favorite lookout. "I knew the Forest Service got real worried about liability; people being injured in one of the old, abandoned cabins. It's similar to the man who constructs a swimming pool and one of the neighbor kids falls in, gets hurt and the owner finds himself liable. The Forest Service was worried, but evidently the Attorney General advised them, I think in 1969, that they really had nothing to worry about; just in time to save Three Fingers lookout."

Harold Engles was inclined to believe that inaccessibility had a great deal to do with Three Fingers surviving the torch. "I really think it was just too much trouble getting up there to do the job. I only wish they could have saved Pugh. It's a darn shame. It was a beautiful lookout."

The tiny cabin on Three Fingers, remote and seldom visited, was left to weather the onslaught of wind, rain and snow. Winter snow would drift around it and the blustery winds would tug at the guy wires while rain warped the walls. Years of neglect began to show: peeling paint, sagging ceilings, and rotting ladders. Inside though, things remained as they had when Harry Tucker last secured the shutters and bolted the door in the early fall of 1942.

Almost thirty years later, in July, I climbed Three Fingers accompanied by my father, Bill, brother, Stu, sister, Liz and climbing buddy, Ruth Thompson. The early morning sun eliminated sinister shadows which had cowed our novice trio two years before. A little more climbing experience didn't hurt either. The chimney looked less forbidding and we easily scrambled to the cabin. The last ladder was missing, necessitating a giant step across. Liz paused for several seconds before reaching for the iron stake and pulling herself to relative safety. Undoing the latch to the front door, we stepped into the dark cabin and back in time 30 years.

The fire finder dominated the tiny room. It still turned easily, but the map showed trails where roads now existed. There were instructions telling lookouts what to do if an unidentified plane was spotted. The lookout was to call in to the main office and say one word, "Flash." Just like Jimmy Olson at the *Daily Planet*. The serious tone of the pamphlet seemed almost comical, but to Harry Tucker working in the lookout during World War II, it was serious business. The old radio, its insides sprung and rusted, its batteries corroded, sat silently on the table next to the door. Hanging from the wall was a kerosene lantern and under the bed on the opposite side of the room were several cans of kerosene which Harry Tucker had loved to lug from Goat Flats. Tucked in the shelves were wrinkled but readable copies of *Life, Time, Colliers* and *Saturday Evening Post*. A *Time* cover headline stated in bold print, "H.G. Wells looks at the New Deal." A *Seattle Times* headline announced that the Marines had landed on Guadalcanal and an advertisement in *Life* had actor Robert Montgomery warning of the perils of pink toothbrush. Pots, pans, cups, a salt shaker and silverware were stacked on another shelf and across the room sat Harold Weiss's canvas chair. No matter where one sat on the lookout's old bed, he would invariably slide to the middle. Wool blankets and an old sleeping bag made it a comfortable resting spot for the climber not concerned with good posture. A quick peek in the attic brought the discovery of a pair of short skis used by the Eastwoods and lengths of thick manila rope. On the table next to the radio was the original lookout register.

Harold Weiss had brought the register up in 1935 and his was the first signature. Each summer, for the next seven years, the lookouts had been the first to sign in. Harold Engles' name showed up frequently as did Charlie Thurston's. Famous Northwest climbers like Fred Beckey, Jack Schwabland, Lloyd Anderson had also checked in. In 1940 Fred Noble had written his name in the book hours before he fell to his death. While glancing through the register, my father looked up and exclaimed, "Peg climbed Three Fingers in 1944." While he was in the service, his sister, an avid mountaineer, had been part of a Mountaineers' outing to the tops of all three peaks.

The register was crowded with Tucker signatures and Tucker witticisms which ranged from the wry to the silly. The register, obviously designed for campgrounds as well as lookouts, had a place for "method of travel" and the Tuckers penciled in such modes as railroad, Western Airlines, truck or pogo stick. After one ascent in the early 1950's, Eileen Tucker wrote "crawled to the top." Rex Tucker, address Dogtown U.S.A., wrote rather shakily that he had been forced to make the trip by mean masters. Another climber claimed to have made the the climb in two left boots. More often though, the comments talked of the "beautiful, perfect, breathtaking or magnificent" views. We were eager to add our signatures to this historical document.

With the shutters closed, the cabin seemed a gloomy place, but with shutters raised, on the east and west sides, sunlight illuminated the room and we could better understand why the lookouts had so enjoyed their summers on Three Fingers. We climbed through the window and lounged on the small terrace on the east side, which Harry Tucker kiddingly referred to as the "back forty". Across from us to the south, separated by a narrow gully, was a shorter spire and on its sheer east face, someone had painted a skull and crossbones and written above it, "Safety First". Next to the painting were the initials, "HT, 41-42".

The glare of the midday sun exposed the cabin's age. It was indeed fragile and in need of more care than the occasional climber could give. While we leaned against the cabin walls luxuriating in the sun's warmth, Harry Tucker and Harold Engles were planning an expedition to repair the cabin.

The idea of maintaining abandoned lookouts was becoming popular with outdoor groups. The Skagit Valley Alpine Club had just taken on the care and maintenance of Hidden Lakes lookout. On Labor Day weekend, 1972, a party of Everett Mountaineers, which included Harold Engles, Kenn Carpenter and his family, Steve and Dorothy Phillips, spent a weekend making repairs on the Three Fingers cabin. A helicopter dropped new ladders, window panes and paint. Several cans missed the mark and splattered on the upper east face. Engles remembers it being a "little like the old days when we first built the cabin. A lot had changed, but the spirit of the people remained unchanged. You know, we almost lost one of the young girls. She was sitting near one of the pane-less windows. Suddenly she pitched backwards. I don't know how many hands reached out to grab her, but it gave us all a bit of a start. It's a long trip to the bottom."

With a new coat of paint and new ceiling supports, the cabin looked ready once again for occupancy. Not content with merely fixing up the cabin, members of the work party returned a few weeks later to fit in place a new shelter at Saddle Lake. The Forest Service again provided materials. The shelter was pre-assembled and helicoptered in pieces to the lake. Despite his satisfaction with the project, Carpenter worried about the shelter and, especially, the cabin. "With easier access to the mountain, I could see every Tom, Dick and Harry making the climb. I just hoped it wouldn't get destroyed."

Carpenter's concern has been shared, fortunately, by almost all who have visited the cabin since its first facelift. Entries in the new register reflect a real concern for the cabin's well-being. Signing in, the hiker becomes more than a visitor. He becomes a steward of the lookout and the history it contains. People who have climbed the mountain often, have little tolerance for those who fail to heed the instructions tacked to the wall: Sweep the floors, close the shutters tightly and take nothing but trash and memories.

In the fall of 1977, shutters left open by hikers were blown off the lookout and down the mountain by fierce storms. On a gloomy August afternoon the following year, my brother, Andy, and I opened the cabin door to find the cabin in disarray. Windows were broken, rain and snow had mildewed blankets and ruined many of the precious vintage magazines. Harry Tucker, already aware of the cabin's plight, was busy rounding up volunteers to repair the damage. One party, including Harold Engles, assessed the damage, prepared a list of materials needed, which the Forest Service agreed to deliver by helicopter. The next weekend, Jim Liming led my father, me, and Jim Gianelli, who was taking his first mountain hike, up the peak. Shortly after we reached the cabin, the wind whipped up and snow began to fall. Jim Liming and I belayed Dad as he edged out on the almost nonexistent north and south ledges to hammer plywood over the windows. It was tedious work and the cold was numbing. But three hours later, as we huddled in our sleeping bags guzzling hot soup, we felt satisfied that the cabin would weather the next winter. Jim Gianelli, who had fallen into bed shortly after we arrived, slept for almost sixteen hours straight. The next morning, we belayed him down the ice-covered ladders and headed quickly back to our cars through the wind, snow, sleet and finally rain. Jim Gianelli then retired forever from the hiking business.

Today the Three Fingers cabin needs another coat of paint, some new shutters, new panes, a new roof, perhaps — the works. But Three Fingers, unlike almost all other fire lookouts in the Cascades, is still standing and, as long as the crushing weight of winter snows doesn't collapse it and hurricane winds howling across the east face don't blow it into Squire Creek, people will be ready to contribute to its upkeep, whether it be sweeping the floor, carrying out trash, painting or pounding nails. The cabin has become more than a shelter for tired climbers. It has become the repository for some of their most precious memories.

Lookout cabin with new roof, 1986.

CHAPTER TWELVE
Wilderness in Your Backyard

The Boulder River Valley is short on views, but rich in sensuous pleasures. Shortly after leaving the car, one is enveloped in dense evergreenery, mist eddying through the sagging branches of Douglas Fir and cedar. The hiker, arching back until the blood rushes to his head and the branches and sky begin to spin crazily, still will not see the tips of these giant trees. Furrowed by years of horse and foot travel, the trail is cushioned by fallen needles and soggy soil.

Rain, in downpours and drizzle, is a daily fact of life in the Boulder River Valley. We hop over rivulets cutting across the trail, but more often we give up and splash through the puddles. Ancient Western Red Cedar loom around each corner and crowd the path. Peeling bark and shaggy branches give them a grizzled look. They are, in fact, the remnants of a magnificent forest which once covered the Puget Lowland. Their musty odor mingles with the wet underbrush, a fragrance that Eddie Bauer or L. L. Bean may someday bottle and sell to people who want to smell like the great outdoors.

Very little light filters through the evergreen cover. It could be pre-dawn or twilight, but it is mid-morning. Green and its various shadings is the dominant color, the only one that seems to thrive in the shadows. A mile up the trail we are as deep into the mountains as a person can get. The sense of isolation from the civilized world, only a few miles to the north, is overwhelming. After four miles of mimicking the course of the river, the trail switchbacks two miles to Tupso Pass.

The snowshoes come out of the pack at Tupso Pass. Ten feet of snow covers the road in early April. Our intention is to reach Goat Flats but by late afternoon we call it quits on a small shelf somewhere below Saddle Lake. We had been following the occasional blaze and electrical conductor hanging in a tree, but all signs disappeared and we are above the trail or possibly far below it. The snow is disorienting and we are glad to find tent space on the steep north slope of Meadow Mountain.

After dinner, we sit in front of the tent trying to figure out where on Meadow Mountain we are. Through snow-laden branches we can see the west ridge of Bullon; at least we think it's Bullon. It could be Whitehorse. Speculation puts us half-way between here and there and eventually conversation drifts into quiet reverie. There are no birds, no breeze, no distant river roar or engine drone. Silence is complete except for my inner voice which excitedly chatters on about the absence of any noise. It is a rare moment in a world where life is increasingly played out against a background cacophony of screaming men and machines. A person finds the quiet strangely unbearable and welcomes the muffled thump of snow sloughing off a nearby branch and flopping to the ground. Almost on cue, we begin talking loudly and the silence slips away on a wind that brushes past our faces. The next morning we give up our quest for Goat Flats and head back to the Boulder. It is almost a relief to leave the snow and hear once again the rush of cold water splashing against boulders and careening downstream. Rounding a corner, wilderness ends abruptly and we are at the car. Minutes later, engine humming, radio blaring, we are on the road headed for burgers and fries at our favorite Arlington drive-in. As we cross the bridge spanning the Boulder, we glance back up the valley which is just around the corner, and, for a moment, it is still again.

****

It is all too easy to become blase about a treasure which sits just outside the picture window, especially if one knows it will always be there. The Puget Sound citizenry has always been able to count on the reassuring presence of the Cascade Range, a constant in a chaotic world. But accumulating changes, out of sight, out of mind, perhaps, wreak irrevocable havoc on our mountains and forests. One morning the populace may wake up to a landscape far less comforting, far less picturesque than it had become accustomed to. Rick McGuire will never take the mountains or forests for granted.

"I've always liked the mountains and Three Fingers is just about my favorite mountain in the whole world", says McGuire, a young conservationist for the Snohomish County Public Utility District. "I spent a lot of time staring at Three Fingers from classrooms at Everett High School, probably too much time. More often than not, I wished I was up there instead of in class.

"I've climbed Three Fingers four times, Bullon once and I love to bushwhack around Mt. Ditney. No one ever hikes there, probably for good reason. It's jungle, but I like it that way.

124

I first hiked up the Boulder in 1975 and I was floored. That forest is ancient. It probably hasn't seen a major fire in over 1,000 years, which is unusual for the Cascades. Such a unique forest and the mountains around it need to be preserved. I was born in Everett, Massachusetts, and moved to Everett, Washington, before high school. Had Three Fingers been in Massachusetts, it would have been set aside as a national park, but so few people around this area are aware of what we have. In 1975, there was a real chance we might lose the Boulder."

The steep-sided Boulder Valley had been spared for decades while valleys around it fell to the ax, but in the early 1960's, the Forest Service set its sights on logging the Boulder River Valley. Brock Evans, a longtime lobbyist for the Sierra Club, hiked up the valley in 1966 and found a proposed road flagged along the trail. Through his efforts, the projected timber sales were halted, but the victory was only temporary. In 1971 while the Forest Service considered areas for possible wilderness designation, the fledgling Boulder River protection Association, headed by Mark Bardsley, John Hutchinson, Fay Ogilvie and Henry Kral, organized a successful letter writing campaign on behalf of the Boulder River. Letters in favor of preserving the watershed and mountains it drained flooded the Forest Service; more were received than for any other area in the United States.

Virgin timber and scenic beauty were not the only compelling reasons for designating the area around Three Fingers as wilderness. Art Ryals, a former Forest Service employee, argued that logging, with attendant roads, would destroy the already fragile habitat of the shrinking mountain goat herds in the area. Ryals had kept a head count for over forty years. His figures indicated that the numbers had almost been halved. He said, "We have the power to destroy this last habitat of the mountain goat in this watershed, but we do not have the power or means to ever restore it. It took the mountain goat thousands of years to evolve into a highly specialized animal that can only and will only survive in a very special habitat.

"He has picked the most harsh, barren and valueless land that man controls. As far as man is concerned, the goat is the most innocuous of all the wildlife. The home he has chosen is in almost all instances useless to man except for recreation. And if all these other factors are removed, he is willing to share his home with us and give to us the thrill and privilege of seeing him scale the impossible cliffs to match his indomitable courage with a habitat that no other creature dares to challenge. I just hope and pray that he will be allowed to follow his centuries old trails and continue to live so that future generations will share the thrill of seeing this beautiful creature in his chosen home."

The Boulder remained in limbo until 1979 when the second RARE (Roadless Area Review and Evaluation) recommended non-wilderness status for the Boulder Valley and the Three Fingers area.

"I first became concerned about the area," said McGuire, "when I found out that helicopters were regularly landing in the Craig Lakes Basin. It is such a remote and beautiful area. I was really ticked off and I couldn't believe the Forest Service would allow logging in the Boulder.

"I revived the Boulder River Protection Association in 1979 and, with the help of some of the original members, put together a media campaign. We made sure the newspapers and TV stations were kept informed about the Boulder Valley situation. We wrote lots of letters and I wrote articles for magazines. I was in college and had the time and energy to devote. We managed to gather quite a bit of support. Both the *Everett Herald* and *Seattle Post Intelligencer* endorsed Wilderness designation. Most importantly, I was able to get Al Swift to take a look at the Boulder River. He had just been elected to the U.S. House of Representatives, and although not an outdoorsman, he was favorably impressed and became our strongest backer.

Congressman Swift, who Joel Connelly of the *Seattle Post Intelligencer* once called a "great indoor man", admits to being a bit of a stranger to the hiking trails of the North Cascades. "I've never been one for a lot of physical exertion, and that has included an ability to avoid long hikes in the hills. It was this viewpoint, however, that drew me to the Boulder River Wilderness area. When Rick McGuire first raised the questions, I was particularly intrigued with that portion of the Boulder River that is both very close to populated areas — just a few minutes from downtown Everett — and can be walked into by everyone from young families with tiny children to older folks who may not be in as good physical condition as Harold Engles. I think that while wilderness which is isolated and difficult to get to is perfectly justifiable, it is the opportunity to provide a wilderness experience for those who are unable, or disinclined to make the dedicated physical commitment necessary for some of the more remote wilderness areas that attracted me to the idea of including Boulder River in the wilderness package the Washington Delegation submitted to Congresst"

Early in 1980 Swift introduced a Boulder River Wilderness Bill in Congress and kept the issue alive in D.C. In 1981, McGuire testified before a Congressional committee regarding Wilderness. "At that point, we realized that action wasn't going to be taken for a couple of years. It was difficult to tell what the outcome would be. The Boulder River Protection Association hoped that the wilderness area would include mountains to the east of Three Fingers, like Dickerman and Forgotten. Swift's bill was somewhat smaller, about 51,000 acres. But, at that point, any wilderness would be a victory.

In 1984 everything seem to come together. The Washington Congressional delegation and Senators Gorton and Evans came up with a plan that would add just over a million acres of wilderness to that already existing in Washington. The Washington delegation was able to work out a plan that they could all live with. "The Washington State Wilderness Bill was a consensus document that was put together by the Washington delegation, a fairly unique occurence," said Swift. "The Oregon delegation was at swords' point and fought a terrible battle on the floor of the house to get its bill through. I simply indicated that one of the musts for any bill was the inclusion of the Boulder River, as Rick and I finally agreed to submit it. I, of course, had some other interests, including some commercially viable timber for the timber industry which is still vitally important to the economy of my district and particularly to many of the little towns scattered throughout. I've never wanted to fly under false colors and not mention that I both contributed to the amount of wilderness and to restricting wilderness from certain areas of important commercial stands. It was a difficult balancing act but I think one that served in the final analysis the variety of interests that exist in the district running from recreation to preservation to economic concerns."

The Boulder River Wilderness area submitted by Swift reflected his belief in balance. It included the Boulder River, Three Fingers, Whitehorse, Liberty, Big Bear and Ditney, but the new 48,900-acre wilderness area seemed designed to avoid taking in too much timber; wilderness on the rocks. The new Forest Service map outlines the new Boulder River Wilderness.

It weaves in and around logging roads cutting up Canyon, French and Squire creeks and much of the land within its boundaries is near or above timberline. The Boulder River is an exception. Buildings are prohibited in wilderness areas, but fortunately the Three Fingers lookout has been exempted.

While it was not as much as they had hoped, friends of the Boulder River had reason to rejoice. In July of 1984, a celebration was held near the Boulder River trailhead. Rick McGuire was one of those celebrating. "Many times I stood on some high ridge of Ditney, Three Fingers or Bullon and looked down into that jungle above the Boulder Valley and wondered if it would be chopped all to hell like Canyon Creek. I spent five years making sure it wouldn't. Now I feel fairly confident it will stay the same. It's nice to think that there will be a bit of a blank spot on the map around Three Fingers, untouched by roads.

"I haven't gone up the Boulder River since our dedication ceremony last summer. I guess it's because I now feel those incredible forests, hidden glens, benches and basins will be there for me later. I spend most of my time in the Skykomish watershed. We may lose such places as West Cady and Troublesome creeks. The Douglas Fir forest is amazing, not as forbidding as the Boulder, but just as primeval. A few of us have put together a loose coalition, The Friends of the North Fork. It seems as if you can't ever relax."

CHAPTER THIRTEEN
A Walk Through Time

At age 85, Harold Engles still climbs mountains. He is exceptional, but many of his peers, in less dramatic style, also breathe life into the tired axiom: "old age is a state of mind". In 1974, at my brother's wedding while walking from the hotel to a reception, I watched in horror as my eighty-three year old grandfather picked up his spindly legs and loped across a four-lane highway in the face of oncoming traffic. The entire family was aghast and glued to the other side of the street, but he didn't think much of it, didn't even mention it. Never mind that he had just recently returned from another lengthy stay in the hospital. It was just the way he went about his life. It was at about this time that my father's mother decided, in her mid-seventies to take a trip unaccompanied around the world on a tramp steamer. That same year I first met Harold Engles and every notion I ever possessed about aging was turned on its head.

Three years ago my wife and I flew home for the holidays. My mother and Gertrude Shorrock met us at the airport. The ground was covered with several inches of slushy snow and more was falling. Mother asked me to drive and for the next two-plus hours we crept along the freeway barely avoiding accidents all the way. Trucks would roar by us, covering the windshield with slush and a few miles later we would find them jackknifed along the side of the highway. It was a white knuckle experience, but Gertrude, who was in her early eighties, loved every minute of it. She exclaimed at the beauty of a snow-covered world and oohed and ahhed appreciatively at our many close calls with careening autos. For her this was an experience to be relished. It was reassuring to have Gertrude along for the ride.

I think it is that unique spirit which inhabits much of this book, whether in the person of Harold Engles or Art Winder. The physical deterioration, which is a fact of all our lives, is a hindrance, a maddening frustration. It would be naive to assume that Harland Eastwood, Jean Fish, Edith Bedal or Robert Craig don't sometimes rage at the injustice of physical aging. There is just too much to be done, whether it be writing a history, traveling around the world, doing volunteer work or tending a vineyard.

Harold Engles is doubly blessed. He has a mind still open to all the possibilities of life and a body still able to explore them. In 1985, two years after this chapter was written, Harold again climbed Three Fingers. He was accompanied by George Freed, Stan Nurmi and Gary Wood. Freed is a longtime hiking companion, one of the members of Harold's over-seventy hiking club. Nurmi and Wood are in their late twenties. Nurmi was impressed with their vigor. "We gave them a fifteen-minute head start and didn't catch them for almost two miles. Harold and George were so much fun and full of energy and tales. That night we had a beautiful sunset. Gary and I brought along a little tequila to celebrate and George and Harold had a few sips. They liked it, too."

Harold later wrote me and said, "That stuff was pretty strong. I almost felt like climbing the north peak before hitting the sack."

Old age often bears the label "The Twilight Years", a bittersweet title. But Harold Engles and others remind us that some of life's most memorable and brilliant moments occur in the golden afterglow of a sunset.

****

Harold Engles's living room, with its picture window opening out on a panoramic view of Whitehorse Mountain, is the perfect setting for his tales of times past. And Engles is a fine story teller, quietly regaling the eager listener with accounts of mountain trails he has traveled, the fires he has fought, the mountain men, the loggers and miners with whom he has worked and called friends and occasionally the men with whom he has tangled. But at age 85 Harold Engles is still a busy man. He has a small farm to tend and trails to hike. He works at both every morning of the year and, entering his ninth decade, Engles is more vigorous than most men half his age. More often than not Engles's stories are told to the listener as he hurries to catch the energetic octogenarian on some mountain trail.

On Labor Day weekend in 1983, Engles returned to Three Fingers. He was accompanied by neighbor Wayne Sizemore, Wayne's friendly dog, Sherpa, and me. The morning of our climb was gloomy, much like the overcast September morning in 1929 when Engles and Harry Bedal traversed the mountain for the first time.

It was hard to imagine the soft-spoken Engles 81 or even 61 as he hoisted his 35-pound pack and shambled up the trail. He led our trio at a steady pace. Sherpa was the only member of our group who chafed, trotting up and down the trail constantly, although he never bothered the animals, at least those he had a chance of catching. Wayne claimed that Sherpa had been taught not to bother marmots, but I remained dubious until the next day when we came to a patch of snow covering the trail. Sherpa, who had bounded ahead, was waiting quietly for us. On the snow, not more than fifteen yards away, sat a nervous and puzzled marmot. I was impressed. Sherpa had not even barked.

Although we didn't race up the path as Harold had on his legendary 35-mile day hikes fifty years ago, there was only one major rest stop during the ten-mile ascent. The miles passed pleasantly as Engles recalled in detail the unique trail building problems on Three Fingers; those amazing stretches blasted out of solid rock high on the mountain. Just below Tin Can Gap, Harold pointed to a naturally terraced switchback he had discovered in 1929. When he and Bedal staked the trail, Engles made sure it wound around that terrace. Harry Tucker had said, "Harold is really proud of that spot and he likes to tell me about it every time we climb Three Fingers. I kid him and ask, 'Harold, isn't this that switchback you found', even though I've heard the story several times before because I know he'll tell me about it. Yeah, he really liked that stretch of trail."

Engles entertained us with a scrapbook's worth of anecdotes. In each meadow, at every bend in the trail, there was a memory triggered and a story recounted . . . The time he came upon a herd of thirty-five mountain goats grazing in a meadow above Goat Flats . . . Old Joe Gerkman, who had drilled holes in the rocks near Saddle Lakes in hopes of striking it rich and had about as much luck with precious minerals as he did with his homemade wine . . . Those young men who had manned the lookout . . . Harry Bedal, barrel chested and hard as the rock he dynamited, the driving force behind the construction of the Three Fingers trail and lookout. Listening to Harold, the past became almost palpable. The gray clouds, lowering, hovered overhead like a lingering memory. Harry Bedal could have been waiting for us around the corner and, sensing the longing in

Engles's voice when he talked of Bedal, you knew he wished he were.

Anecdotes were interspersed with advice along the trail. During the first half of the century, outdoorsmen like Engles were without the fancy equipment that today eases aching backs and feet. Harold made many of his packs, clothes and lanterns. Used Model T tires wrapped around a pack frame had provided the type of comfort that hikers pay $100 for today. A candle and carefully-cut coffee can made an excellent lantern that was windproof, too. Harold remarked, "We often had to get by on ingenuity although that didn't always work. We used bacon grease as mosquito repellant back in the early days. I never figured out what good it did. The mosquitoes must have died from too much cholesterol." Twenty-six years ago Harold bought his first and only metal frame pack. A couple of years ago he added a padded hipbelt and periodically he would proclaim, "This is the second best invention after the wheel."

Engles also advised Wayne that if he wanted to keep his wife happy when he went hiking without her, he should "Do something nice around the house when you get home, without even being asked; wash the dishes, mow the lawn, and that will be good for another hike. The more chores, the more hikes."

We all laughed and Wayne thanked Harold for the advice and Engles added, "I'm not sure my wife would be too happy if she heard me talking like this." It was a perfect day for a tape recorder or a memory as good as Harold's, neither of which I possessed. But the hours passed quickly and by early afternoon we were crossing the snow fields below the lookout. Sherpa loved the snow, but Harold has developed a healthy respect for steep snow and gladly let Wayne and me kick steps. It was the only time that day he relinquished the lead.

The horse trail which was carved to within several hundred feet of the lookout is occasionally littered with the remnants of the construction; a length of metal used to winch lumber from the trail to the south peak, a stovepipe left at the high camp, telephone wire snaking through the rocks along the trail. Useless and a bit of an eyesore, they nonetheless evoke nostalgia and summon up visions of Ed Towne hanging over the edge of the south summit, slowly winding the winch and keeping his eyes closed . . . sure-footed Mabel, leading a string of mules up the airy trail . . . Harland Eastwood and Bob Craig uncoiling the 80-pound bales of wire, scrambling up the rocks to stretch wire from Tin Can Gap to the cabin.

Eight hours after leaving the car, we rounded a corner and caught our first close-up glimpse of the cabin. Gazing at the old lookout perched on the south peak one could readily see why Engles and Bedal chose that spot for a cabin. But the thought of actually building it still defies imagination. With the clouds turning dark and fearsome, we didn't linger on its (im)practicality. Although battered by a half-century of snow, wind and rain, the cabin still provides comfortable lodging. The ladders, replaced in 1972, made the final ascent easier for all except Sherpa, who had lost enthusiasm for the climb and was hauled up under Wayne's arm. After opening the cabin, we relaxed on the rock terrace on the east side until chilly winds drove us inside. Wayne and I stemmed down a chimney to take a look at Bob Craig's restroom. It was spacious but vulnerable to some wicked winds which whipped across the east face. Harold had no desire to inspect it. He said he'd done enough foolish things in his youth.

The clouds eventually engulfed the cabin, but we spent an enjoyable evening hearing more stories about the lookout, its construction and the men who had worked there. The wind blew all night and I was reminded of Harold Weiss who had recalled big gusts lifting the cabin off the ground. One had to adopt a fatalistic attitude, lie back and enjoy the soothing sound the wind made as it whistled through the cracks. Shortly before dawn, the wind stopped momentarily and in the lull the cabin was lifted slightly off the ground and jolted back to terra-not-so firma. Harold remarked excitedly, "That was an earthquake". Returning to Snohomish that evening, I found that, indeed, we had been awakened by a tremor felt all over the Northwest. I comforted myself with the thought that the cabin had survived several earthquakes over the years.

The cabin, buffeted by the elements, has managed to remain standing for over five decades. It sags a bit in the middle and has buckled in other spots. The bed and tables are a bit wobbly, but climbers have been good about following an admonition written in the register, "Leave the cabin cleaner than you found it." Before leaving we spent an hour housecleaning and making minor repairs.

The summit was still shrouded in mist when we began the descent. Sherpa was even more reluctant to make the trip down

Harold Engles on upper Three Fingers trail, 1983.

the ladders and exhibited a facility for clutching the rungs and hanging on for dear life (I was reminded of several occasions when I had been gripped with the same fear). The young dog was much more comfortable on snow, jumping, sliding and rolling down the upper snowfield. We adopted a more cautious approach. Harold seemed confident during the descent, commenting several times that going down "beat the heck out of going up."

We hurried down the trail, hoping to beat the grim-looking clouds advancing from the south. As we passed the shelter at Goat Flats, which has been reduced to a pile of rotting logs, Harold talked about the Forest Service. He is unhappy with the changes which have effectively stripped the agency of people who actually hike the trails and maintain them. He senses that the men who work for the Forest Service are becoming more distanced from the lands they manage. Rare is the district ranger who travels the trails like Harold Engles did in the 1930's and '40's. The intimacy with the hills is gone, making it easy to view the forests as a product to be packaged rather than a resource to be treasured and managed with care.

Engles sees little relation between the Forest Service of forty years ago and today. What it has gained in efficiency, he believes, it has lost in spirit. There are no Harry Bedals, Harland Eastwoods, Harry Tuckers or Robert Craigs working in today's Forest Service. "We worked hard, but you know, there was always the opportunity for a little fun. Without that it wouldn't have been as satisfying. In the last years, for me, there wasn't much of that. When money's involved, with timber sales and the like, the whole emphasis changes."

At Saddle Lake we met a group of young men heading up the mountain. It had already begun to drizzle and they had only covered seven of the eleven miles. It was well after one p.m. They seemed to be inadequately dressed, but they pressed on. We wondered at their judgement but didn't say anything. We merely exchanged glances. After they had passed, Harold said, "It was bad enough getting down from the cabin. I don't think those boys have any concept of what's ahead. I felt like talking to them about going on in this weather, but they're young and I don't think they would have listened."

One couldn't help but recall another group of climbers heading for the summit of Three Fingers on a rainy day 54 years ago. The boys, with their new boots and flashy packs, bore little resemblence to Harry Bedal and Harold Engles.

The rain beat us to our cars by about four miles and the last couple of miles were quiet ones. The rain was dribbling down the inside of my rainjacket and I, along with Wayne, began to pick up the pace. It was not comparable to wading down Squire Creek in darkness, but it was a small misery and I began to hope for the car around each corner. The last mile seemed like a sprint, but when Wayne and I turned around at the cars, Harold was not far behind.

Our good-byes were short. Harold figured he would forego his regular three-mile morning hike. After all he had another mountain hike planned in two days and he wanted to be rested. The evening before in the cabin, Harold had admitted he was glad to be on top but he wasn't sure he'd ever make the trip to Three Fingers again. Almost in unison, Wayne and I chimed in that we thought he'd be back. Harold smiled and said, "You're probably right."

Harold Engles, 84, on Green Mountain trail, 1986.

CHAPTER FOURTEEN
The Circle is Complete

Tin Can Gap is a fine place to rest and catch breath lost on the switchbacks below the notch. It provides the first dizzying view of the old fire lookout. The south peak juts up almost nine-hundred feet from the Three Fingers glacier, the oddly angled bow of a ship cut loose from the stern and listing badly to the north. On top rests the cabin. By any stretch of the imagination, save that of Harold Engles or Harry Bedal, the cabin has no business being where it is. But it is, and with the help of a few committed friends of the cabin, it looks as if it will be there for another fifty-five years.

On this warm August afternoon I am ready for a break in the action. My cramping calves and lead-heavy thighs demand it. Three young men in their late teens are sprawled against their sleeping bags. One of the bags is the old cotton kind replete with pictures of Roy Rogers, Dale Evans and the rest of the chuckwagon gang. They don't have a tent.

One of the trio asks if I am going to the cabin. When I nod yes, he says, "The place is packed, man, and they're taking the roof off."

That's good news. I drop my pack and fish around for my binoculars. I can see someone on that exposed roof. I hope they have a secure belay. The roofer is either Pat Tucker or her husband, Bruce Weide, halfway through their month-long sojourn on the mountain and putting the finishing touches on a project conceived shortly after Harry Tucker's death in 1984 — the restoration of the Three Fingers lookout cabin. My contribution to the project has been minimal. I envy them their month on the mountain.

Lowering the binoculars, I catch sight of two climbers leaving the trail for the snowfield that ascends to the summit. The orange pack can only belong to Jim Liming who has served as organizer, fund raiser and catalyst for the project. By late afternoon we will all meet at the cabin. I can hardly wait.

Before I leave Tin Can Gap I mention to the three hikers that the gentle afternoon breeze may become a gale after sunset.

"Hey, no sweat. We're set," says one of the guys as he pulls two bottles of Jack Daniels from his pack.

"We've got tunes too," says another, and he muscles out of his pack one of the largest stereo tape decks I have ever seen. Hurricane force winds will be no match when they crank up the volume. I laugh when I think of another trio who brought up a tiny portable radio on the mountain seventeen years ago. They didn't have a tent either.

A few hours later I catch up with Liming and another Jim, Jim Haynes, just below the ladders. Bruce Weide is pounding on the last cedar shake when I drop my pack at the cabin's front door. He and Pat, along with old friend, Mary Boyer, are in a mood to celebrate. Prior to the roof raising, they had shored up the sagging foundation and rebuilt the south wall. It calls for champagne, but the jug of cheap domestic wine I have carried up will probably do in a pinch.

Pat Tucker, standing at the door, smiles and shakes my hand. She seems taller than her father, but that smile is Harry's and the eyes, like Harry's, exude warmth and promise a little mischief in the bargain. When she speaks I hear Eileen and I am drawn back to the Tucker home. Spartan, like the cabin, and plunked down in a beautiful natural setting, it was the site of many memorable conversations. Harry and Eileen always mentioned that it would be great if I got together with their daughter and son-in-law; I would like them. Shaking hands with them at the cabin, I know I will.

Bruce is gregarious and straightforward. I am hardly settled on the bed before he starts grilling me about my book. He is working on his master's degree in creative writing at the University of Montana and his comments are perceptive and constructive. He seems awfully serious until he finishes one story and lets loose with a raucous, infectious cackle that fills the room and spills out and down the east face. We are all convulsed and rarely stop laughing after that.

A huge length of coiled climbing rope lays in a corner of the cabin. Bruce explains that he has been poking around the east and north faces below the cabin and has found all sorts of things including a few tunnels. He invites me on a trip but I decline. I immediately regret my decision when he drops over the edge. For the next hour he crawls all over the rock and brings back a treasure, one of the old army cots that mysteriously disappeared a few years ago. It is salvageable. All it needs is new canvas. Jim Liming makes a note and promises to have some material sent up before the month is out.

For six months Jim has made sure that the pieces of the project fall into place. He is a truly modest man and deflects all praise directed toward him to other people: Carol and Mike Pinneo, Pat and Bruce, Wayne Ledford, Harold Engles and volunteers from the Everett Mountaineers. But without Jim's guiding hand, Pat and Bruce know they would not have been on the mountain this summer giving the cabin a long-needed facelift. Bruce has said, "We were really thinking about the summer of 1987. I never dreamed that Jim would take the ball and run with it like he did."

The evening clouds obscure the sunset, but nobody seems to mind too much. It could be the wine, but I tend to believe it is the companionship and the knowledge that something special is being preserved. For Jim there is the satisfaction of knowing all the preliminary work has paid off, not necesarily a sure thing one month ago. Pat and Bruce are, for a month, living just as Harry did for two summers, sharing it with friends like Mary. For Jim Haynes, the climb of Three Fingers transcends all other trips into the mountains. He will never forget this evening. I just feel honored to be in the presence of such fine folk, old friends and new.

Neither Jim nor I are anxious to leave the next morning. Goodbyes are long and heartfelt. I keep looking back at the cabin every so often and, just above Tin Can Gap, Pat, Bruce and Mary give us a big whoop. We yell something goofy back at the tiny figures standing in front of the cabin, salute with our ice axes and drop down the trail and out of sight. As we make our way to Goat Flats Jim says, "You know, in the grand scheme of things, the Three Fingers project is small potatoes, but I think years from now I will still look back on this project as one of the highlights of my life."

****

In 1980, shortly after their marriage, Pat Tucker and Bruce Weide, with a couple of the Tucker cousins, climbed Three Fingers. It was Bruce's first ascent of the mountain. "I had just finished instructing Outward Bound courses, still retained a bit of the sheep-herding instinct, and here were Pat and her cousins hopping all around the outside of the cabin as if there were no cliffs. I retreated to the cabin and was leaning against the south wall when it gave slightly and I was given a bird's eye view, between the cracks, of the Squire Creek Valley twenty-five hundred feet below. I spent the rest of the day as close to the middle of the cabin as possible."

The cabin was in sorry shape. The repairs in 1979 had only been temporary. Pat and Bruce knew that without major repairs, the cabin could collapse at any time. The idea of a major restoration began to percolate in their minds. In 1984 the Tucker clan was shaken by the death of Harry. In 1985 his brother Jim died. That same year Denae Rideout, a cousin, died in a freak avalanche during a family climb of Whitehorse. Out of the sadness grew a resolve to see the lookout restored to its former glory. In so many obvious and intangible ways, the cabin signified family.

In the winter of 1986 Jim Liming received a letter from Pat Tucker.

> My father, Harry Tucker, was always interested in maintaining and preserving the Three Fingers lookout cabin, and I feel the same way. This summer my husband, a cousin and I made a list of needed repairs and took detailed measurements. It seems like if some rather extensive, but in no way impossible, maintenance is not done in the next few years, the lookout will deteriorate rapidly. Major needs include a new shutter and fastening system, a wall bracing and roof.
>
> I think that if enough people could be gotten together to volunteer time and money, the job would not be a burden on anyone. My cousin and husband are both very good at "seat of the pants" carpentry and are willing to take a few weeks off to do the work up there. What's needed more than people to help up there is people willing to make a trip or two to carry materials up. And of course we need people to pitch in a few dollars. A ballpark figure would be $1,000.
>
> We really aren't able to commit ourselves to this summer before March. Actually the summer of 1987 would be better, but if the momentum is here for this summer, we can do it.
>
> I wondered if you'd be able or interested in helping with logistics. Please think about it and let me know. I'd like this to be a fun experience and not a hardship on anyone. If there's a core of committed, responsible people, it seems like there's the potential for a lot of fun and a feeling of accomplishment.

Jim Liming was, indeed, able and interested. He had spent part of his youth in Oso, a tiny community west of Darrington. His father had worked at Summit Timber Company in Darrington for many years and had been a fire lookout on Mount Pilchuck in 1939. On many a Saturday Jim would get out of bed at dawn and drive up to Darrington with his father. There was always a little work to be done at the mill, but the rest of the day would be spent on some mountain trail along the Mountain Loop Highway. Jim had always had a special place in his heart for Three Fingers. He tried to make a point of getting up the mountain every summer. Jim responded immediately to Pat Tucker's letter.

> Your letter arrived yesterday. Your plans to restore the roof, shutters and walls at the Three Fingers lookout cabin are the best news I've heard in a long time. For some time now I've been hoping that the cabin would last long enough for my young kids to enjoy it on future trips with me. It's more than fifty years old now. Maybe, with some work, it will last another fifty years.

A vice president at Rainier Bank, Liming quickly set up a Three Fingers' repair account, deposited a $200 check Tucker had included with her letter and added $200 of his own. He got in touch with friends of Three Fingers and shortly had exceeded the $1,000 goal.

Pat Tucker had also contacted Harold Engles who spoke to the Everett Mountaineers in hopes of enlisting their support. The response was favorable. In March Liming met with committee chairmen, Carol Pinneo and Jerry Thompson, along with members of the Mountaineer's Conservation Committee, who quickly determined that faced with a potential avalanche of Forest Service paper work, the project would be too much.

"The rest of us", said Liming, "decided to go for it. We decided I would raise the money, acquire the material and get it packed up to Tin Can Gap. The Mountaineers would make it all "legitimate" by getting a special use permit and they would get the material from Tin Can Gap to the summit.

"On June 16, we had a work party at Carol Pinneo's. We made shutters, cut the lumber and established dates for the campaign. On July 13, Dad and I delivered the material to his sister, Loretta and her husband, Wayne Ledford, in Darrington. Wayne, a professional packer, had offered to haul the shutters and tools to Tin Can Gap."

After an auspicious beginning, the project almost foundered on the deadfalls that left the Meadow Mountain trail almost impassable. On a rainy Wednesday, July 16, Wayne Ledford, along with Chuck and Wilma Jenkins tried to pack the materials in, but the trail was a mess. Carol and Mike Pinneo who had accompanied the pack train to take pictures, reported there were at least ten windfalls blocking the trail to Saddle Lake, some firs measuring three feet in diameter.

Jim Liming didn't want the project postponed or, worse,

abandoned. "I decided I would make a one-day commando raid with a chainsaw (in a wilderness area?) and called Carol and Mike. They were a bit apprehensive, being conscientious Mountaineers, but agreed that if I started early in the morning, a group of Mountaineers would follow later and just do the hand labor, moving the logs they would find already cut. I called Harold Engles who wasn't sure he could make it but offered his cross-cut saw and wedges. I also contacted Stan Nurmi, who was planning a trip in the Pickets (a remote range in the North Cascades) but I convinced him that carrying the tools (that Pat Tucker had sent from Missoula) to the cabin would be far more rewarding. Finally I called my dad and asked to borrow some tools. He surprised me and said, 'Do you want me to help?' We hadn't been out in the woods for years, he's 69, and although I was pleased to have his company, I was a bit worried.

"Friday night, before the early morning "commando raid", Harold called and said, 'You know, I talked to George Freed and what time do you want us?'"

"Hell, I had to come clean and tell this retired Forest Service veteran I was consciously going to break the law. He floored me by replying, 'That doesn't bother me at all. Chain saws? I won't be the one using them. Besides, if someone from the Forest Service is up there, just act dumb as a post.'"

"I asked Harold if they would confiscate my rented chain saw. He laughed and said, 'You're big enough that I don't think they'd try.'

"Early Saturday, my dad and I drove to the trailhead. Harold and George were already unloading Harold's cross-cut saw from his VW Beetle. He had to remove the handles from each end to make it fit inside. It was razor sharp, all wrapped in cloth to avoid ripping his upholstry. He told me, 'You know, when we used to pack these things, we didn't use the handles — too much nonsense to carry — we just put a nail through the hole in each end of the blade and used 'em that way.'

"I was still feeling guilty about getting Harold involved so I suggested that Harold and George drive up to the Tupso Pass trail, hike in to Saddle Lake and work their way down the Meadow Mountain trail to meet Dad and me. 'That way you'll be a long way from those chain saws.' After awhile they agreed and drove up the road.

"Dad and I went right to work. One hundred yards up the trail we found an old, punky hemlock. It was like cutting butter. Another hundred yards farther was the Incredible Hulk. It was a big, strong fir, blown down and laying across a switch-back, actually blocking the trail in three places. Our thirty-inch saws were only half its diameter and, worst of all, where we first encountered it, it was hanging fifteen feet above our heads, a potential widow maker.

"We tried various partial cuts and angles, worked on it for almost an hour with little success. I was watching my watch, looking up at the tree, worrying about everything and then we got Dad's saw stuck under two or three tons of vertically hanging Douglas Fir. It was stuck solid. I got an idea, took a peavey, a lumberman's hook, climbed up the slope and straddled the log on the horizontal part, just before the break. I hooked the peavey in the end of the widow maker and, while Dad worked with his leverage from below, we started rocking . . . 'Heave-Ho . . . Heave-Ho . . . Heave-damnnnn! The log rolled down the slope and I rolled after it. I broke my glasses, scraped the skin off my back and cut my hand. I landed on the lower part of the trail, thinking my day might be ending about two hundred yards from the car.

"But the trail was clear, at least that far and, as we picked things up and headed for the next challenge, we were startled to see George walking up the trail toward us. He said, 'How's it going?'

"We said, 'Fine, this one gave us a little trouble, but we got it.'

"He said, 'I'm sorry to say the horse died.'

"'Oh my God, Harold?'

"'No, the Volkswagen. And Harold just had it in to the mechanic the other day. He asked me to walk back and find you before you got too far away.'

"Dad decided he would mosey on up the trail and do what he could and I would go back with George and drive my car up to his. It was almost nine a.m. and the Mountaineers were expected in an hour. I left my pack and chainsaw in the trail and told my dad to be careful.

"George and I drove about four miles before reaching Harold's VW. I have a VW and had my tools, so for about forty-five minutes we farted around with it. Nothing doing. We decided to tow it, but there wasn't much to tie my chain to. I dug around, found two carabiners, didn't have much faith in them, but they held for eighteen miles almost all the way to the paved Mountain Loop Highway. At that point, a car came around a curve toward us, at about fifty miles-per-hour (probably the Mountaineers). I hit the brakes, an automatic reaction. Harold, at the end of our fifteen foot tow chain, did likewise. But we didn't do it exactly the same. The carabiners broke and the chain got wrapped up under Harold's car. On its way, the chain punctured the brake line and his left front wheel was stinking with splattered, hot brake fluid.

"After patching things up, we headed down the Mountain Loop and as I neared the top of Robe Hill I looked in my rear view mirror at Harold. I couldn't hear him yelling, but I could see him yelling. His brakes were completely gone. He was pulling for his life on the parking brake, turning it left and right, anything to make me stop. I stopped, we all got in my car, and drove to Granite Falls for a wrecker. It was almost one p.m. before I returned to the trail. My dawn commando raid had blown up in my face, but I was determined to salvage the day. I hustled up the trail, met my dad who had cleared about two miles up the trail before being overtaken by the Mountaineers. After lunch Dad headed home and I headed back up the trail. I didn't have as much energy as I'd had earlier in the morning.

"Along the trail I passed eight or nine freshly-cut windfalls. About four p.m. I decided to take a break. I had hardly settled in when I heard voices coming my way. 'Hey, hey, hey, good work, nice going!' The Mountaineers had cleared all the way to Saddle Lake and were on their way down. The tools were on their way to the cabin. Success all around. We walked the four miles out together. I had travelled twelve miles and worked on only the first two logs, within two-hundred yards of the car.

"That evening, at my parent's house, Dad said he had thoroughly enjoyed the day. It had been good, hot July weather, the woods fresh, time had passed slowly. The people were 'nice kids'."

With the Meadow Mountain trail cleared, the problems for the packers were eased considerably. The following week Harold Engles and George Freed drove Harold's newly repaired VW up to the Tupso Pass trail and worked on the last tricky spot in the trail, just above Saddle Lake. They rebuilt a section of puncheon that edged out over a small cliff. There were a few muddy sections early on where some of the horses sank up to their knees and one mule tumbled off the trail on the way up Meadow Mountain, but Ledford's next trip up was relatively uneventful. Over the next two weekends the Mountaineers, spearheaded by the Pineos, hauled all materials, including almost a month's supply of food, up to the cabin. Pat Tucker and Bruce Weide had everything they needed.

For the next month the Three Fingers cabin was home to Pat and Bruce. Blessed by exceptional weather, the twosome had little trouble completing work on the cabin. They were helped by an almost steady stream of friends and relatives: Eileen Tucker and Pat's brother Bob, who hadn't been up Three Fingers in twelve years, his son Bill, cousins, Phil Tucker, who brought fresh scallops, Cris Rideout from Alaska and uncle, Dave Tucker, his wife, Kitty, and daughter, Debbie. Another Tucker uncle, Tommy, hiked up to Goat Flats with his crew. Friends, Mary Boire, Jeff Cooper and Bill Hunger all put in a week's duty at the cabin.

"Hunger was around to help put the new roof on," Bruce said. "A practitioner of Yogananda, a blend of all religions, he meditated an hour every day during sunrise. One day, while we were on the roof shingling, I asked him 'Are you truly happy?' The question was hardly out of my mouth when the carabiner attaching him to the rope slipped on his harness. It had happened to me before. For a second you see your life pass by. Actually you slip maybe two inches, but it feels like forever. Bill was caught by surprise and yelled out, 'Shit for brown gravy!' He'd gone absolutely white. I couldn't help laughing. I asked him again if he was happy and he replied, 'Very, very happy. You know, according to my beliefs, the last words you say are what you become in your next life.''

During the month the cabin was jacked up and its foundations reinforced, the south wall rebuilt and the floor leveled. A new coat of paint was applied and the shutters attached, perhaps the most difficult job of all. Pat and Bruce found ways to open the shutters from inside so that people will not be as likely to leave them up. Bruce said, "I never got used to hanging off the side while putting the shutters up. There is so much exposure and each shutter took so much time. Each of them needed a custom cut and drilling holes with no leverage was like drilling into outer space. But luck seemed to be on our side. As we were tightening the very last shutter bolt, it started to snow."

Besides the big jobs, they found time for little projects. Bruce

Pat Tucker and Bruce Weide at lookout cabin, 1986.

Reconstruction volunteers, left to right, Mary Boyer, Bruce Weide,
Jim Haynes, Jim Liming, Pat Tucker, 1986.

built a bookshelf to take the place of a missing window and the fire finder was fixed and oiled.

All was not labor for the work party. Bruce spent many hours exploring the cliffs that bound the cabin. He and an old climbing partner ascended the middle and north peaks, retracing "the route Harry Tucker probably used to make those amazing one-hour north peak ascents. One of the strangest and most rewarding aspects of our triple header climb was that upon reaching the south summit, we were home. It felt funny to top out and also be done, no return. We were where we were supposed to be. It was a novel and great feeling."

Shortly before the end of their stay, Bruce, Pat and cousin, Cris Rideout were called upon to rescue a hiker who had broken his leg sliding down the third snowfield above Tin Can Gap. It was not the first accident on Three Fingers, but for the first time in forty-four years there was somebody in the lookout who could come to the aid of an injured climber.

Bruce said, "Cris had gone for a walk in the mist and came upon this fellow named Doug and his partner, Andy. Cris returned to the lookout for Pat and me. We loaded our packs and headed down. While stabilizing Doug, a figure appeared in the mist atop the snow field. After a lot of yelling in the mist, ('Help, I'm scared. I need an Outward Bound instructor!') I figured it was my climbing buddy, Jeff; we had worked Outward Bound courses together. So Doug lucked out. He had two O.B. instructors familiar with mountain rescue, a registered nurse (Pat) and Cris, whose specialty is good old common sense. The next morning we joined forces with the Snohomish County rescue team to pull off the technical evacuation. I sensed that we wouldn't be needed beyond Tin Can Gap so we politely took our leave. You know, if it was in the cards for Doug to break his leg in the mountains, he couldn't have picked a better time. Plus, the whole thing was an exciting challenge for us. Who doesn't love playing hero?"

Pat and Bruce locked up the cabin four weeks after they had arrived. Bruce said, "The moon had started growing again, just as it had when we arrived and I felt loath to be leaving. I told Pat, 'If something like heaven exists, then I just got a sneak preview.' I could think of no other block of time when I felt so content, complete and useful. I got to live on top of a mountain, an environment which I can but briefly visit in most circumstances."

For Pat the stay was a fulfillment of a dream. "As long as I can remember, I had always wanted to spend an extended period of time at the lookout. Unlike most dreams fulfilled, this exceeded expectations. The emotions elicited are rather difficult to put into words. I felt very close to Dad; he was everywhere, had touched everything. At the same time I was finally saying goodbye — he's not really coming back — so there were lots of tears as well as euphoria. Mac, you know as well as anyone how much he loved that place."

The project was the completion of a circle in the lookout's history. The restoration was done in the old style, much the way Harold Engles did it fifty-years ago. And Harold was there to lend a hand fifty-five years later. And for one month there was a Tucker manning the lookout. Curiously absent was the Forest Service which gave its tacit approval but little else to the project.

Darrington District Ranger William Butler said, "At times, facing reduced budgets, the Forest Service has made concerted efforts to remove structures that were no longer necessary to the administration of the Forest and that were costly to maintain. Even though Three Fingers has not been used as a fire lookout since about 1943, it has not been removed due to the efforts of the Everett Mountaineers to complete the required maintenance."

Although "no longer necessary to the administration of the Forest", Butler admitted that there are other reasons for preserving the Three Fingers Lookout. "In recognition of its historic significance, the Forest is in the process of nominating Three Fingers, along with several other lookouts on the Forest, to the National Register of Historic Places. Because of this, and strong public sentiment, our current objective is to continue to allow the Mountaineers or subsequent user-groups to maintain the building until such a time as they are no longer willing or it is destroyed by natural forces."

At the moment the Everett Mountaineers are committed to maintaining the cabin. In September members repaired the trail up to Saddle Lake. The future looks bright. In late September Jim Liming hiked up to Squire Creek Pass and said "The cabin absolutely shone. It looked brand new." Harold Engles also hiked up to the Pass and reported that the cabin stood out like a gem on the skyline. If only Harry Tucker could see it now.

THREE FINGERS

To get there
  walk up through a dark forest
    where moss drips down to decay
  Then up to a lake saddled between two mountains
      (You can find a good place to sleep there,
          a nest between some well placed fir
            at the edge of a cliff
          with a good view of the glacier
            and the Three Fingers

From there, follow the ridge east,
    past elvish canals that cut through meadows
        where gnomes chockol ground squirrels
           and back away with sheepish grins.

There are little kettle lakes up higher
    in a large alpine meadow.
        And after the first frost in early fall,
          if the sun is out,
          they are nice to swim in.

Up there, nothing stops the wind
    that comes in from the ocean
        ignoring tides
        and punishing trees that stand
          bent, stunted and flagging east

Keep following the ridge up into the high country
    where there is just rock, lichen, sedges and ice;
    and mountain goats lick rocks,
        that you pissed on, for the salt.
Next, cross the top of a steep glacier whose
    titan groans can be heard
        as you climb the last of the route
    up to the south spire — that stands there
        as if it were imagined by an Iowa corn farmer.

And atop this is the Lookout,
    a vertical half-mile drop behind it,
        a thousand feet off the front.

Tonight, when everyone else is asleep,
    I will go out.
There will be a full moon and clouds from the coast
    rolling inland farther and farther . . .
        until the world becomes mountain tops
        sticking up out of clean cotton.

I will think, "I am better than others for being up here."
    I will know this isn't true,
        but beneath my thoughts I will know it is.
    Then I will go back inside the Lookout to sleep,
        the moon interfering with my dreams.

                    — Bruce Weide